STEWARD LEADER MEDITATIONS

Fifty Devotions for the Leadership Journey

R. SCOTT RODIN

KINGDOM LIFE PUBLISHING

Steward Leader Meditations

Copyright © R. Scott Rodin, 2016

All rights reserved under International and Pan-American Copyright Conventions. Reproductions or translation of any part of this work beyond that permitted by section 107 or 108 of the 1976 United States Copyright Act is unlawful. Requests for permissions should be addressed to:

Kingdom Life Publishing
P.O. Box 389
Colbert, WA 99005

To contact the author, write to:
R. Scott Rodin
21816 N. Buckeye Lake Lane
Colbert, WA 99005
U.S.A.

All Scripture quotations, unless otherwise indicated, are taken from the Holy Bible, New International Version, NIV. Copyright © 1973, 1978, 1984 by International Bible Society. All rights reserved.

ISBN 978-0-615-31076-3

Printed in the United States of America

*This collection of meditations is dedicated to my father,
Bob Rodin, who went home to be with
his Lord earlier this year.*

*My father was the consummate steward leader
who saw the very best in everyone and lived
at that sublime intersection of humility and courage.*

I love you, Dad.

Steward Leader Meditations are also found
in the online course, Becoming a Steward Leader.
To find out more about the course go to
www.thestewardsjourney.com/courses

Contents

Foreword 9

Introduction 11

Part I
From Owner to Steward

Meditation #1 – Knowing the God Who Leads 17

Meditation #2 – Why the Trinity Matters to Leaders 20

Meditation #3 – The Certainty of the Steward Leader 23

Meditation #4 – Leading in His Image 26

Meditation #5 – A Leader in All Spheres 29

Meditation #6 – Leadership as a Gift. 32

Meditation #7 – Set Free to Lead. 35

Part II
From Two-Kingdom to One-Kingdom Leadership

Meditation #8 – Selling It All 41

Meditation #9 – Trust That Changes Us 44

Meditation #10 – Fear Not. 47

Meditation #11 – Leading with an Undivided Heart. 50

Meditation #12 – Reliance on God's Faithfulness 53

Meditation #13 – The Power of Testimony 56

Meditation #14 – Throne of Grace 60

Part III
From Stagnancy to Intimacy: The Heart of the Steward Leader

Meditation #15 – Are You Convinced? 65

Meditation #16 – Have You Died? 69

Meditation #17 – Defining Success 72

Meditation #18 – Fruit That Lasts 75

Meditation #19 – The Myth of Godly Drivenness 78

Meditation #20 – The One Thing 82

Meditation #21 – Prayer as Means and End 85

Part IV
From Distraction to Balance: The Image of the Steward Leader

Meditation #22 – The Leader in the Mirror 91

Meditation #23 – Who Are You? 94

Meditation #24 – Neither Pride Nor Doubt 98

Meditation #25 – Finding Our Feet 102

Meditation #26 – The Applause of Nail-Scarred Hands 107

Meditation #27 – Humble on the Steeple 111

Meditation #28 – A Leader of No Reputation 115

Part V
From Means to Ends: The Relationships of the Steward Leader

Meditation #29 – Finding Your Fellow Traveler 121

Meditation #30 – Leading the Unlovable 125

Meditation #31 – Looking at the Heart 129

Meditation #32 – The Relationships That Define Us 133

Meditation #33 – Responses That Surprise 136

Meditation #34 – Stand Still and Listen 140

Meditation #35 – You Find Out Who Your Friends Are 144

Part VI
From Complacency to Nurture:
The Work of the Steward Leader

Meditation #36 – Digging Out a Deadly Root 149

Meditation #37 – Whom Will You Serve? 152

Meditation #38 – Ruling in His Image 156

Meditation #39 – The Essential Tension in Creation Care 160

Meditation #40 – Work and Worship 164

Meditation #41 – Redeeming the Time 168

Meditation #42 – The Vocation of the Steward Leader 172

Part VII
From Apathy to Warrior:
The Battle of the Steward Leader

Meditation #43 – Prepared and Engaged 179

Meditation #44 – Two-Handed Leadership 183

Meditation #45 – Naming the Enemy 187

Meditation #46 – Proclaiming Freedom 190

Meditation #47 – Struggle and Victory 193

Meditation #48 – Set Free to Lead 196

Meditation #49 – Victory Begins with Surrender 200

Meditation #50 – The Charge of the Steward Leader 203

Foreword

Early in my tenure as president of Eastern Baptist Theological Seminary, a colleague of mine handed me a little book entitled *Leadership Prayers*. At the time I was navigating my way through some particularly treacherous waters, and as I scanned the table of contents I found that almost every subject had meaning for me in the challenges I was facing. In this wonderful book, Richard Kriegbaum provides leaders with a treasure full of candid dialogues with God on the issues that challenge us the most. I am humbled and delighted that Rich has agreed to write the introduction to this collection of Steward Leader Meditations. I pray that this book might provide even a fraction of the blessings I know his has for leaders globally.

The fifty meditations in this collection reflect my work on the theology of the steward leader. The layout is divided into seven sections, which reflect the seven keys that are the foundation of steward-leader theology. Each of these keys unlocks a chain that binds and burdens leaders, keeping us from the freedom and joy that is meant to be ours as steward leaders. These chains represent the bondage of ownership, control, spiritual stagnancy, misplaced identity, manipulative relationships, complacency toward resources, and apathy in the face of the spiritual battles before us. I pray God works to unbind you and loose these chains as you engage with the meditations in each of these seven areas.

These meditations and prayers also reflect the four spheres

of relationship that define us as human beings and children of God—namely, our relationships with God, with our selves, with our neighbor, and with the created world. These are the media through which leaders employ their craft. Relationships are the source of our greatest challenges, and how we steward them will define our legacy. I have woven thoughts on our work in these four areas of relationship throughout these meditations. I believe the key to whole relationships in each is our ability to be true steward leaders that have been set free to lead in obedience and joy. I pray you discover that freedom in the pages ahead.

Finally, I've offered a suggested action step with each meditation. My hope is to supply you with tangible ways to experience this freedom for yourself. I believe if you will try these steps, they will provide an added blessing to these devotions.

It is my prayer that you will find a meditation that speaks to your situation at every place along your leadership journey. You can work through these sequentially, or you can choose meditations that strike you as being especially poignant for the context in which you are leading. Either way, may the Holy Spirit indwell each word, touch your heart, and equip and inspire you for the high and holy calling of the steward leader.

R. Scott Rodin
April 2016

Introduction

Richard Kriegbaum

You may have seen it and cringed: A parent acting as though they owned their child. "How could you do this to me?" they wail, as though the child belonged to them and existed for their happiness.

By contrast, how beautiful it is when wise and healthy Christian parents view their child as a gift that the creator God has entrusted to them. They see themselves as stewards of his divine vision and purposes for that child's life. They understand that the child belongs first and above all to the God who made that child, and the child exists for a joyful and intimate relationship with God and for service in Christ's kingdom.

Perhaps because the distorting heresy of human ownership has become the almost universal assumption of contemporary culture, it is much harder for us to recognize this mind-set when the legal owner or CEO of an organization brazenly declares or demonstrates by their behavior that "this is my company and I can do whatever I want with it." Or perhaps you have heard a subtler explanation by a Christian business leader who measures his company's success solely by how much net profit can be produced for donations to support Christian missions.

In his book *The Steward Leader*, Scott provides a comprehensive and compelling rationale for leadership that transforms people, organizations, and communities by removing the heavy yoke of bondage carried by an owner leader. That ownership burden and its concomitant small view of God can be replaced by the light and joyful freedom of the steward leader. Steward leadership depends on a theology of creation by an all-knowing, all-powerful, and truly good triune creator God.

As I studied Scott's book *The Steward Leader* and used it in teaching, mentoring, and consulting, I realized that he and I had assembled many of the same sources and had independently come to similar conclusions about leadership and the nature of healthy organizations. *The Steward Leader* describes in rich theological principles and practical detail the alternative to the onerous worldview and corporate culture of the owner leader. He describes what every Christian leader in every organization—whether it is overtly Christian or not—would (or should) want. He presents a convincing description of what steward leadership is and why it is the only model of leadership that every sincere follower of Jesus should study and implement.

But if it is so obviously true and transformative, why is this leadership framework not rapidly becoming the universal model of organizational development? The answer is that understanding what this leadership model is and why it matters so much is not enough to make it happen. Even reaching the point of sincerely wanting it and being willing to let go of all the old ownership ways of believing, thinking, and behaving are not enough for the needed transformation to become reality.

What becomes painfully clear is that for the leader and the leader's organization to achieve the enormous benefits of a pervasive corporate culture of stewardship under the one-kingdom reign of Jesus Christ, the Christian leader must experience a profound and pervasive personal transformation. *Steward Leader Meditations* provides a detailed plan and guidebook for the long, difficult, painful, and sometimes costly pilgrimage to becoming a Jesus-following steward leader.

The *Steward Leader* explains the *what* and the *why* of steward leadership. *Steward Leader Meditations* explains *how* to actually do it, how to make the leadership transformation an internalized reality in your life. Each of the two books is effective and valuable alone, but they are also a powerful pair that inform and enhance each other. The need for two such different books derives from the challenging reality that leadership is a complex field and no one resource can meet all the needs of every leader in every situation. Nevertheless, the dichotomy of the owner mind-set and the steward mind-set establishes a firm metafoundation of applied theology for making meaning in all other leadership frameworks.

There are more than a hundred understandings, models, and definitions of leadership. The simplest and most universal definition is "a leader has followers." That simplicity on the other side of complexity took many decades to evolve. People in an organization recognize leadership as a differentiated role that some person must play for the welfare of everyone involved. The most common view of why people follow a particular person, and thus make that person a leader, is that the person is able to do certain necessary things that a leader does. A leader is someone who does what a leader needs to do.

But the premise of *Steward Leader Meditations* is that for a person to consistently *do* what a true steward leader must do, they must *be* a certain kind of person. The being precedes and determines the doing. Becoming a different kind of person with a different mind-set is profoundly spiritual work by the Holy Spirit, who requires the committed engagement of the person who wants to change. The process involves the practice of spiritual disciplines that form new habits of the heart and mind.

As you move through these fifty meditations, you will follow a carefully designed sequence of learning and personal and professional development. You will look at each person, each situation, and each outcome differently. You will trade constraints for creativity, anxiety for confidence, fear for faith, and weariness for energizing intimacy with God. You will see your organization differently when you experience the joyous freedom of being a steward leader that God has appointed in an organization that God owns with outcomes that only God controls. You will approach your leadership differently.

Each of the fifty daily meditations includes a biblical text, a short and specific key thought, a teaching that explains and illustrates the key concepts, a very practical and creative action plan—something you can actually do and learn from—and a prayer, a beautiful and powerful guided conversation with God. The meditations are arranged so you can do one each day for a week, for seven weeks, with a closing summary meditation on day fifty. Or you can work on one each week and devote a year to becoming a true steward leader. They'll work well for your personal journey, but you can use them with your leadership team as a group devotional as well.

However you do it, if you sincerely complete this fifty-day process, you will be a different person and a different leader. But that will just be the beginning of your journey. When you finish these meditations, including the fifty prayers, this book will also have become a point of reference to which you will return often. I am confident these steward leader meditations will change you like they continue to change me. All you need is an open heart and mind for what God's Spirit wants to do in your life and in your organization as part of his kingdom, in which he owns everything. In his kingdom we have the wondrous privilege of being stewards of every relationship: with God, with ourselves, with our families (in healthy balance with our work), with our neighbors (including our followers), and with the world God created. It is not ours. It is all his. Our joyful privilege is to be faithful and wise stewards as we follow and as we lead.

Part I

From Owner to Steward

The challenges of leadership are undoubtedly complex. Yet some of the principles that lead to real success in leadership may be surprisingly straightforward. I believe the simplest is the choice we make between an owner orientation and a steward mind-set. Owner leaders and steward leaders provide fundamentally different types of leadership. From our definition of success to our identity to our management style to our attitude toward resources, the choice we make between these two leader-views will shape who we are, the way we lead, and the fruit of that leadership.

My prayer is that God's people will be compelled by scripture to embrace and pursue the life of the steward leader. This first set of meditations is designed to help you on that journey.

Meditation #1

KNOWING THE GOD WHO LEADS

Philip said, "Lord, show us the Father and that will be enough for us." Jesus answered: "Don't you know me, Philip, even after I have been among you such a long time? Anyone who has seen me has seen the Father" (John 14:8–9).

KEY THOUGHT

We can live with a profound sense of peace because we know the heart and the nature of the God who created us.

TEACHING

Two young boys were sitting outside of a principal's office. They were about to be called in and held accountable for a violation of school rules. As they pondered their fate, the first boy lamented, "I'm so scared. I know what I did was wrong, but I've heard this principal is really tough. I'm afraid he might be harder on me than what's fair. What if he wants to make an example of me? I just have no idea what to expect."

The second boy looked over at him and replied calmly, "You're right, he is tough, but he's also fair. We're both going to get what we deserve but nothing more. I can promise you that."

The first boy looked back at him with surprise. "This is the toughest principal in the state—how can you be so sure he'll be fair to us?"

The second boy replied confidently, "Because he's my dad."

There is a profound difference between knowing about someone and really knowing them. The first boy knew a lot about the principal, but the second one knew him as his own father. Which of these describes your relationship with God? Do you just know a lot about God from what you read in scripture, what you hear in church, and what others say about Him? Far too many people in our world have a lot of information about God, but they can't say they truly, personally, and intimately know Him. That's a recipe for living in fear.

Read again these words of Jesus from John 14. He's encouraging, almost pleading with the disciples to understand that just as they love Him, trust Him, have confidence in Him, and would follow Him anywhere, so they should love, trust, and have confidence in their heavenly Father. Jesus came to reveal to us the heart of God. He states clearly to Pilate that he came to bear witness to the truth (John 18:37). That truth is the great news that the God who created us and sustains us is the God who loves us, sent His Son for us, and desires that we know Him, love Him, and have a relationship with Him.

Do you know the Father? Do you really know Him—intimately, personally, deep down in the core of your soul? There's no trick to it. It's all there for you in Jesus Christ by the power of the Holy Spirit. Don't go another day of your life without the absolute certainty of God's love for you and His invitation to draw near to Him with confidence, for His throne is a throne of grace (see Hebrews 4:16).

Action

Create space in your life to get to know God on a deeper level than you are currently experiencing. Cancel a meeting, turn off your laptop, silence your phone, and find a quiet place. Open scripture and begin with a prayer: "Lord, I want to know you more intimately. I will draw closer to you, believing and knowing that you will respond by drawing even nearer to me." Then read, pray, and spend time being quiet in God's presence. Listen, keep your heart open, and expect Him to speak. Practice this discipline every day for this first week and see by the end if you have not been drawn into a richer relationship with Him.

PRAYER

Read John 17:20–26 and turn it into your own prayer to the Father, in the name of His Son and by the power of His Spirit.

Meditation #2

Why the Trinity Matters to Leaders

I have revealed you to those whom you gave me out of the world. They were yours; you gave them to me, and they have obeyed your word. Now they know that everything you have given me comes from you. For I gave them the words you gave me, and they accepted them. They knew with certainty that I came from you, and they believed that you sent me. I pray for them. I am not praying for the world, but for those you have given me, for they are yours. All I have is yours, and all you have is mine. And glory has come to me through them. I will remain in the world no longer, but they are still in the world, and I am coming to you. Holy Father, protect them by the power of your name, the name you gave me, so that they may be one as we are one (John 17:6–11).

Key Thought

We praise God that He is Father, Son, and Holy Spirit, for if He were not triune in His nature, He could never reveal himself to us and we would never know Him, our selves, or our purpose in life.

Teaching

Mention the doctrine of the Trinity to any believer, and you will likely get a sigh and a roll of the eyes. "Who can understand it?" most people reply. Pastors try to describe the Trinity like an egg (shell, white, and yolk, but one egg) or like water (liquid, solid, and vapor, but one substance) with little effect. It is one of those teachings that we believe passively, but because we can't understand it, we tend to think that it really has little consequence for the way in which we understand scripture, God, and life. Nothing could be further from the truth. I could go as far as to say that the doctrine of the Trinity is the single most important belief we have as followers of Jesus Christ. Without it, our entire faith crumbles like a house of cards. The reason is really quite simple.

If Jesus Christ is not fully God, then He could not (1) reveal God, (2) bear the sins of the world on our behalf, (3) reconcile us to the Father, (4) defeat death, or (5) promise us everlasting life. Yet He proclaimed himself to be fully God, one with the Father. And it is in the name of the Father, and the Son, and the Holy Spirit that people are baptized into the one Church of Jesus Christ.

We don't have to understand it; in fact, we should praise God that we have a God whose very nature is beyond our human comprehension. But this we do know, and this we must celebrate—because God is triune, He is able to reveal himself to us, die for us, redeem us, and call us back to Him for eternity.

> Holy, holy, holy, Lord God Almighty
> All the earth shall praise thy name in earth and
>   sky and sea
> Holy, holy, holy, merciful and mighty,
> God in three persons, Blessed Trinity.[*]

ACTION

Do a web search on the words "images of the Trinity" and notice all the ways that artists throughout the ages have tried

---

[*] "Holy, Holy, Holy," written by Reginald Heber, music by John B. Dykes.

to depict the tri-unity of God. As you do, give thanks to God for His triune nature and all that it means to you as a follower of the Son, in worship of the Father by the power of the Spirit.

Prayer

O most holy Trinity, almighty God, we adore you, who gives life and vigor to every creature and who sheds light eternal where there is darkness. We offer you our hearts, our souls, and our whole being, today and in the days to come, that we may offer perfect praise and love to your glorious name. Amen.

O Father almighty, we thank you wholeheartedly for all the blessings and graces you have so generously given us then and now.

O merciful Christ Jesus, wash away our sins with your most precious blood. Feel the beating of our hearts and make them like your own. O dear Jesus, wipe away our tears and pardon us for our sinfulness. Be with us, O Lord, until our dying day, that we may be worthy of your mercy and forgiveness.

O Holy Spirit, our guide and inspiration, lead us to the right path. And if, on our way, we encounter difficulties and trials, do not allow us to fall or lose hope. Grant us the graces we need daily that we may also share our blessings with our fellow travelers. And when the time comes, O Holy Spirit, lead us to the place that is secure, full of joy and eternal peace. Amen (author unknown).

Meditation #3

The Certainty of the Steward Leader

Though I have been speaking figuratively, a time is coming when I will no longer use this kind of language but will tell you plainly about my Father. In that day you will ask in my name. I am not saying that I will ask the Father on your behalf. No, the Father himself loves you because you have loved me and have believed that I came from God (John 16:25–27).

Key Thought

In God's self-revelation to us, we can know with certainty that He is "for us."

Teaching

There is an episode in *Star Trek: The Next Generation* ("Who Watches the Watchers," season three, episode four) in which the *Enterprise* crew encounters a planet whose citizens come to believe that the ship's captain, Jean-Luc Picard, is God. The episode culminates with one of the believers aiming an arrow at the heart of crewmember Counselor Deanna Troi. Some of the people think "God" wants them to kill her, while others do not. They question how they are to understand "God's will." At that pivotal moment, Counselor Troi proclaims, "That's the problem with believing in a divine being—you never really know what they want you to do." That line was the whole message of the episode. Even for followers of Jesus Christ, there is a small bit of rather painful truth in those words.

Do we really know God well enough to know His will? Can we really trust Him? How do we know that the loving God of today will not change to a wrathful God tomorrow? What certainty do we have that we can know God's will with confidence and trust His heart without exception? Rephrasing Counselor Troi's question, how do we know for sure what it is that God wants us to do?

Our only trustworthy source for answers is God's incredible love for us, which we know through His self-revelation to us via Jesus Christ. Hear these words from Romans and claim them for your own. They provide the absolute certainty, the unquestionable confidence, and the unequivocal answer to the questions of God's nature, love, mercy, and grace toward us.

And we know that in all things God works for the good of those who love him, who have been called according to his purpose…what, then, shall we say in response to these things? If God is for us, who can be against us? He who did not spare his own son, but gave him up for us all—how will he not also, along with him, graciously give us all things? (Romans 8:28, 31–32)

Make no mistake, my friends, the God that has been revealed to us in Jesus Christ is our Creator God, who is for us, and has been from all eternity.

ACTION

Write on a piece of paper, "If God is for me, who can stand against me?" Carry it with you or put it in a place where you can see it consistently throughout your day. Meditate on that thought as you face the issues and challenges of the week. How does that word of assurance impact your outlook on your day? What does it say to you about God, life, work, suffering, and joy? Write down your responses on the other side of the card and then decide how you will remember this lesson throughout the rest of your life.

PRAYER

Gracious heavenly Father, I thank you that I can have the certainty of knowing that you are for me. I claim at this moment the truth that you love me, you created me just as I am, you walk with me every moment, and your grace flows to me without limit. Lord, I should be overwhelmed by all of this, but so often I forget it or downplay it or simply take it all for granted. Instill in me the wonder of your love. Let me know again the deep peace that comes from the assurance that if you are for me, no one can stand against me. Overwhelm my timid and tired spirit with your courageous and triumphant Holy Spirit. I pray with David that you will restore unto me the joy of my salvation. In everything I think, say, and do this day as a leader, let me be influenced by your presence, guided by your hand, and secure in your love for me. In Jesus's precious name, amen.

Meditation #4

LEADING IN HIS IMAGE

It is by grace you have been saved through faith (and that is not from yourselves; it is the gift of God)—not by works, so that no one can boast. For we are God's handiwork, created in Christ Jesus to do good works, which God prepared in advance for us to do (Ephesians 2:8–9).

Key Thought

We were created in the image of God as His covenant partners to engage in our lives' great work in and through relationships.

Teaching

God has work for us to do! That is the clear message of Ephesians 2. We were created specifically to do the work that God prepared for us to accomplish during our years on earth. Our lives have meaning, purpose, and a job description. And God fashioned us for this work. We are His handiwork. Isn't that amazing? God specifically designed and created you and me with the skills, temperament, and makeup to accomplish exactly the tasks He prepared for us to do before we were even knit together in the womb. Incredible!

From the moment of our conception, we were given a clear vocation that stays with us until the moment God calls us home. That vocation is to live fully as a child of God and a follower of Jesus Christ. Jobs may come and go, careers may rise and fall, but our vocation never leaves us. We bear God's image in this world as we live out that vocation in relationship. Our Creator God is Father, Son, and Holy Spirit—one God in three: a dynamic, interdependent relationship in unity. We reflect the image of our triune God when we willingly engage ourselves in the relationships that surround us.

In every action we take as leaders, we are reflecting God's image in relationship. This is our work, our calling, our special privilege, and our vocation. It is the purpose for which we were created, and when we live it out, we draw nearer to our Creator God than at any other time in our lives.

How will you bear His image in the way in which you lead and in the relationships that surround you? If you are truly God's handiwork, what has that prepared you to do for Him?

Action

If your vocation is uniquely yours from birth to death, you should be sure you know what it is. Take a moment and, in one sentence, write a job description that puts in your own words the vocation God created you to carry out. Remember, you are a child of God, created to love Him and live with grace and truth in all the relationships that surround you. Use this thought, along with Romans 8, and develop a brief description of your vocation. Then share it with members of your leadership team to learn what they affirm about you, and what you may add as a result of their input.

Prayer

Gracious Lord, I am amazed at how unique you have made me. I lose sight of that so often. Thank you for reminding me that I am your handiwork. I am created for a purpose, carefully crafted for a role and the work that you have designed for me. Help me know what that is. Open my eyes and my heart to see clearly the vocation to which you have called me. Don't let me miss this, Lord! I want to live and lead to glorify you—with all my heart, soul, strength, and mind. Align my heart with your intention for my life and work as a leader and help me pursue it with my whole being. As I bear your image in my work, help me lead so that the world will really see you in all I say and do. I want to do the work you created me to do, Lord. Help me see it and do it with obedience and joy. In the name of my Savior and Lord, Jesus Christ, amen.

Meditation #5

A LEADER IN ALL SPHERES

So God created mankind in his own image; in the image of God he created them; male and female, he created them. God blessed them and said to them, "Be fruitful and increase in number; fill the earth and subdue it. Rule over the fish in the sea and the birds in the sky and over every living creature that moves on the ground." Then God said, "I give you every seed-bearing plant on the face of the whole earth and every tree that has fruit with seed in it. They will be yours for food. And to all the beasts of the earth and all the birds in the sky and all the creatures that move along the ground—everything that has the breath of life in it—I give every green plant for food." And it was so. God saw all that he had made, and it was very good (Genesis 1:27–31).

KEY THOUGHT

The creation story paints for us an amazing picture of a people created for whole, meaningful, and loving relationships in four spheres.

TEACHING

This text from Genesis is a beautiful example of all four levels of relationship for which we were created. Can you identify them? Begin by considering that God desired to create a creature that would bear His image in a way that was unique among all the other creatures of the earth. The first sphere of relationship was established in God's loving creation of humanity. By bearing God's image, we were given the unique responsibility to fill the earth as a continuation of God's creative work and to rule over it in the same loving, nurturing way that God rules over us. We bear God's image when we live into our relationship with Him and carry out the work He created us to do. Inherently connected to that first relationship sphere is the second: God's creation of humanity also allows for our relationship with self—fully understanding who we are, why we were created, and what our vocation is on this earth.

Can you determine the third and the fourth? The third sphere of relationship has to do with our caring for one another. God put Adam and Eve together with the command that they be fruitful and multiply and fill the earth. We bear God's image as male and female, and we carry out His command by leading our community in ways that glorify Him and further the work of His kingdom. The fourth, and not least, relationship is the one we have with the creation itself. We were created to rule lovingly, to tend the garden, and to subdue the earth in the same way that our Creator loves, cares for, and subdues us.

These four relationships are the sum total of the purpose for which we were created. It's really a beautiful scene. The life of a steward leader is marked by an intimate relationship with God, peace with ourselves, loving service to those we lead, and tending God's beautiful creation through a faithful use of His provision.

How does your leadership reflect wholeness of relationship in all four of these spheres?

Action

Do you see yourself as having been created for all four of these areas of relationship? Do you take some more seriously than others? The enemy will seek to attack us in our area of weakness. Take a moment to consider in which sphere you struggle the most. Write it down and follow that with a one- or two-sentence commitment you will make today to work against whatever it is that is keeping you from experiencing fullness and joy in this sphere.

Prayer

Lord, you are amazing! You created me in such an incredible way. I want to know and experience the fullness and richness of life in all four of these spheres. I want everything you have created for me. However, I confess that I fall so short of this abundant life. I have written down the sphere of relationship where I struggle the most. You are fully aware of my struggles here. So now is the time to lay this before you and submit it fully to you. I am tired of struggling with these relationships, and my only way out is through you. I give it all back to you. Heal me, change me, encourage me, and empower me to live and lead as your child in all four spheres. I know you want me to have life and have it abundantly. I know you want me to lead as a faithful steward leader. I yield myself to you to bring forth in me what is necessary for me to lead in this way. Take all of me, Lord. Everything in my life and work in every sphere—it is yours. I am yours, fully, completely, and eternally. In Jesus's name, amen.

Meditation #6

LEADERSHIP AS A GIFT

The gift is not like the trespass. For if the many died by the trespass of the one man, how much more did God's grace and the gift that came by the grace of the one man, Jesus Christ, overflow to the many! Nor can the gift of God be compared with the result of one man's sin: the judgment followed one sin and brought condemnation, but the gift followed many trespasses and brought justification. For if, by the trespass of the one man, death reigned through that one man, how much more will those who received God's abundant provision of grace and of the gift of righteousness reign in life through the one man, Jesus Christ (Romans 5:15–17)!

KEY THOUGHT

Everything that was lost in the fall was redeemed in Christ, and as such it has been given back to us as a gift.

TEACHING

In our last devotion we looked at the four spheres of relationship in which we were created, and we were amazed at the beauty of each. Unfortunately, we know from Genesis 3 that when sin entered the world, it brought brokenness to all four spheres. We must not take this lightly. The level of brokenness ushered in by sin was absolutely devastating to God's beautiful creation. There was not one thing that God created that was not tarnished, twisted, and distorted by the fall.

This sets the cross of Christ in an even more amazing light. Christ came not only to redeem our relationship with God but also to buy back for us our relationship with ourselves, our neighbor, and creation itself. Paul's words in Romans make this clear, and I love the emphasis on that triumphant term, "how much more…!" Paul's point here is to make sure we understand that even though sin brought incredible devastation across all spheres of relationship, the cross of Christ blew that sin out of the water. It not only restored what was lost, but, even more importantly, it overwhelmed sin, death, and destruction, ushering in the kingdom of God and pointing us toward an amazing eternity.

Now we face the moment of decision. If everything God created for us was lost in the fall, and if it was all bought back for us with the precious blood of Jesus, then we must confess that the entirety of our life—every relationship in every sphere at every moment of our existence—is an incredible gift. And if all of life is a gift, then we can only respond by living as stewards. That one word defines us more than any other word in scripture. We are not owners—we are grateful stewards who have been given the most amazing gift in the history of the world.

How does your leadership today reflect your understanding that all of life is a gift? How will you lead your organization in ways that reflect your gratitude for this gift and your call to be a faithful steward of all of life?

Action

We learn from childhood to say "thank you" when we are given a gift. Practice that courtesy with God today, remembering that everything we experience in every sphere of life is a gift from Him. Spend your day thanking Him for your relationship with Him, with yourself, with your neighbor, and with His creation.

Fill your day with praise and thanksgiving, honoring the Giver of all things.

PRAYER

Gracious and loving heavenly Father, thank you, thank you for everything in my life. I forget that it is all yours. Forgive me for pretending that I am the owner and acting like I am in control. All of that just brings me pain and stress and distances me from you. I renounce my claim of ownership of everything in my life and work. With great joy I proclaim that everything is yours! Thank you for drawing me close to you through the blood of your Son, Jesus. Thank you for giving me my identity as your child and my vocation as a citizen of your kingdom. Thank you for my coworkers and the opportunity to love and serve them. Thank you for this amazing creation and the high honor of nurturing it and caring for it. And thank you for not only being the Creator and Owner of all things but also for being the lavishly generous and loving Giver of all I need, every day and for eternity! I love you! In Jesus's name, amen.

Meditation #7

SET FREE TO LEAD

Do not store up for yourselves treasures on earth, where moths and vermin destroy, and where thieves break in and steal. But store up for yourselves treasures in heaven, where moths and vermin do not destroy, and where thieves do not break in and steal. For where your treasure is, there your heart will be also (Matthew 6:19–21).

Then he said to them all, "Whoever wants to be my disciple must deny themselves and take up their cross daily and follow me. For whoever wants to save their life will lose it, but whoever loses their life for me will save it" (Luke 9:23–24).

KEY THOUGHT

We are called to the life of the faithful steward, rejecting a false sense of ownership and being set free by the total surrender of the one-kingdom steward.

TEACHING

In light of our last devotion, the idea of storing up treasures for ourselves on earth should seem ludicrous. We have made the claim that all of life in every aspect is a gift from God. We defined our role on this earth as stewards of these precious gifts. Imagine the audacity of grabbing these gifts for ourselves and claiming some kind of counterfeit ownership, as though we were their Creator and the redeemer. Absurd! But that is the constant siren call of the enemy, the idea that we as leaders can grab control and claim ownership over those things that have been so lovingly given back to us through the blood of Jesus Christ.

- We now stand at the crossroads of perhaps the greatest leadership decision of our lives.
- Will we follow the values of the world around us and pretend we are owners, or will we embrace the mantle of the faithful steward leader?
- Will we succumb to the temptation to focus our leadership on growing our own kingdom, amassing the trappings of leadership, consuming more than we need, and claiming that somehow it is all an indication of God's blessing in our lives, or will we choose to "lose" this counterfeit life that we may lead the way God intended us to lead?
- Will our measurement of success in our life be based on our income or our outflow?

This is where two worldviews collide. It is where the values of the kingdom of God run directly counter to the world's standards and norms. It is where following Jesus Christ requires sacrifice that yields a different and more meaningful kind of abundance than we have ever known. It is the narrow gate, the path of obedience, the way of the cross.

In the end it is absolute freedom. We conclude on this note. Playing the owner leader will always reward us with bondage. Embracing our call to be steward leaders will always set us free. If you are facing fear, stress, anxiety, doubt, despair, sadness, or discouragement, my question for you is this: Do you want to be free?

Then this is your journey—the journey of the faithful steward leader set free.

Action

I challenge you to take this action seriously. See if it doesn't have a profound and lasting effect on you and the way you lead. Get the deed to your house, the title to your car, your investment portfolio, your bank account statements, your retirement account documents, and the birth certificates for each of your children (if you don't have some of these items, find things that represent your ownership of the stuff in your life). Place all of these things on the table; just pile them up and sit and look at them for a moment. Then hold hands with your spouse, children, or friends, and pray the prayer below. This is your opportunity to feel what it is like to relinquish the counterfeit ownership of people and things (which you never really have anyway) and experience the freedom of the faithful steward.

Prayer

Lord, this is so hard. The world around me drives me to look for security in balanced budgets and financial strength, to measure my worth by what I earn or the money we raise, and to trust my future to how much we have stored up for ourselves. I confess that everything I call mine has become a source of bondage for me. I confess that I place my security and look for happiness in things rather than in you. Forgive me, Lord, and please, set me free! I claim today that you are the sole owner of everything in my life and my organization in all four spheres. Drive from my heart the thirst for ownership and the hunger for control. Give me a heart that desires only you, one that is satisfied with obedience and content with simplicity. It's all yours, Lord. Help me remember that every moment of every day and help me live and lead with the freedom that results from that simple yet transformational statement. Set me free, Lord, set me free! In the name of the one who came to set us free, indeed, Jesus Christ, our Lord. Amen.

Part II

From Two-Kingdom to One-Kingdom Leadership

―――※※※―――

The journey from the orientation of owner leadership to the call of the steward leader requires that we identify and name the "second kingdom" that we have allowed to be constructed in our lives. This is represented by all the things over which we seek to retain control, or at least the image of control. It is the sphere of our life and leadership where we use the word "mine." It may be articulated as "my ministry," "my church," "my business," "my people," "my congregation," "my programs," "my plan," "my board," "my donors," etc. On a more personal level, it may come out as "my time," "my reputation," "my ideas," "my money," or "my stuff." In whatever fashion, we all have second kingdoms over which we like to play the lord.

These alien kingdoms produce fruit in our lives in the form of fear, stress, anxiety, discouragement, and even despair. The operative description for what we experience as second kingdom builders is "bondage." And that's just where the enemy wants us—pursuing control over our second-kingdom stuff and being immobilized in the process. If he can't make us unfaithful, he will settle for rendering us ineffective.

The remedy for second kingdom building is absolute surrender. It requires us to step off our thrones, abandon our quest for control, and yield everything back to God. It's His anyway. As we do, the chains of bondage will fall and we will be set free to lead in freedom and joy. That is the journey of the steward leader.

These next seven meditations are designed to help you on that journey of surrender and freedom. This is heady stuff, so don't journey this week without the coverage of prayer by your friends and family. We are heading into the greatest battle in our lives as leaders. And in this battle, victory begins with surrender.

※

Meditation #8

SELLING IT ALL

A certain ruler asked Jesus, "Teacher, what must I do to inherit eternal life?"

"Why do you call me good?" Jesus answered. "No one is good except God alone. You know the commandments: you shall not commit adultery, you shall not murder, you shall not steal, you shall not give false testimony, honor your father and mother." "All these I have kept since I was a boy," he said. When Jesus heard this he said to him, "You still lack one thing. Sell everything you have and give to the poor, and you will have treasure in heaven. Then come, follow me." When he heard this, he became very sad, because he was very wealthy (Luke 18:18–23).

The kingdom of heaven is like treasure hidden in a field. When a man found it, he hid it yet again, and then in his joy went and sold all he had and bought that field (Matthew 13:44).

KEY THOUGHT

What is your response to Jesus's invitation to embrace the kingdom of heaven and follow Him?

TEACHING

I have always found it rather unnerving to read these two texts side by side. The contrast could not be sharper. In the first, Jesus offers the wealthy young ruler treasure in heaven. He invites him into the kingdom of God as a fully submitted follower of Jesus.

He offers him freedom, joy, and the opportunity to begin his own journey with Jesus as a faithful steward. When this wealthy man compared the value he had placed on his own riches, "he became very sad."

No doubt he understood just what was being required of him. And he walked away contemplating the price of the journey from his love for temporal trappings of earthly wealth to a surrendered embrace of the riches of heaven.

How striking it is to move from this story immediately to Jesus's parable about the man who is out plowing a field when he happens upon a treasure whose value is beyond his wildest dreams. This treasure is so precious to him that he immediately does the exact thing that the rich young ruler refused to do. He "sold all he had" in order to purchase that field and realize that treasure for himself.

This is the decision that faces us every day. Being a one-kingdom steward leader requires nothing less than the total surrender of everything in life to Jesus Christ. Why would we do such a thing? Because knowing Him, following Him, and serving Him is of inestimable value. When we embrace our call to be citizens of the kingdom of God, the things of this world have no hold on us. We gladly turn over all of our life and our leadership to Him for the opportunity to know that one incredible treasure.

When you look at your life, your leadership values, and the decisions you make in your leadership role, do they bear witness to the first story or the second? Sadness or joy—one of the two will mark our lives today as a direct result of how we answer that question.

ACTION

In both stories there is the idea of selling everything you have. What would it look like in your role as a leader to sell everything you have in order to follow Jesus, to claim for yourself and your organization the treasure of heaven He offers? Take the challenge by completing this sentence:

Jesus, today I commit to sell everything I have and follow you. For me that means I will:

PRAYER

Take my life, and let it be,
Consecrated, Lord, to thee;
Take my moments and my days,
Let them flow in ceaseless praise,
Let them flow in ceaseless praise.
Take my hands, and let them move,
At the impulse of thy love;
Take my feet and let them be,
Swift and beautiful for thee,
Swift and beautiful for thee.
Take my voice, and let me sing,
Always, only, for my King;
Take my lips, and let them be,
Filled with messages from thee,
Filled with messages from thee.
Take my silver and my gold;
Not a mite would I withhold;
Take my intellect, and use,
Every power as thou shalt choose,
Every power as thou shalt choose.
Take my will, and make it thine;
It shall be no longer mine.
Take my heart; it is thine own;
It shall be thy royal throne,
It shall be thy royal throne.
Take my love; my Lord, I pour
At thy feet its treasure-store.
Take myself, and I will be,
Ever, only, all for thee,
Ever, only, all for thee.*

- "Take My Life and Let It Be," written by Frances Ridley Havergal in 1872, music by Henri A.C. Malan.

Meditation #9

TRUST THAT CHANGES US

Trust in the Lord with all your heart, and do not lean on your own understanding (Proverbs 3:5).

KEY THOUGHT

We choose every day in what (or in whom) we will place our trust. It cannot be divided up among several recipients. It is either solely in God or it is not.

TEACHING

There is an old joke about the man who fell over the side of a cliff but was able to stop his fall by grabbing a small branch. As he dangled over the chasm, he looked to the heavens and cried out, "Is there anyone up there who can help me?" Three times he called out, and no one answered. Suddenly the heavens parted, and the voice of God rang out, "I will help you, but you must trust me. I want you to let go of the branch." The man looked down to the ravine below him, considered his options, and then looked back to heaven and yelled, "Is there anyone else up there who can help me?"

So it is in our walk with God. We ask for help, and He responds with an invitation but always requires a step of faith, an act of ultimate trust in Him. In almost every case, trusting God requires us to take steps that seem illogical, countercultural, and uncomfortable. That is the nature of faith and trust. Our text from Proverbs reminds us that trusting God often requires that we set aside our "own understanding." That is, we will be required to reject the way we would do it and embrace wholly the direction in which God is calling us. Adam and Eve faced exactly that choice. They were given the opportunity to enjoy the overwhelming beauty and abundance of the garden God had created for them. All that was required was that they trust God and not eat of the one tree that grew in the center of the garden. That was it. "Enjoy all I have created for you, and trust me that you do not need or want the fruit of the forbidden tree."

We know how the story ends. How about for you? What step of faith, what act of trust is God asking of you? Will you set aside your own understanding and trust in Him? Even if it means letting go of your branch?

ACTION

This is time for absolute honesty with yourself. Complete this statement: If I absolutely, completely, and unreservedly trusted in God for my organization, our finances, and our future, there is one thing I would do differently today:

___

___

Now that you have named it, what will you do about it?

PRAYER

Gracious Lord, I confess that I love to cling to my own understanding. Letting go and trusting you is so very difficult for me. I pray for faith to take this step that you are calling me to take today. I know how different my life and leadership would be if I really trusted in you for everything, and I want that life, Lord. I'm tired of compromising my faith and placing conditions on my trust in you. I want to be all in, holding nothing back, completely submitted. I can't do this on my own—I know because I've tried and failed so often. But I claim the promise that through you I can do all things. So give me the strength and the courage to step boldly in the direction that you're calling me. Fill me with a new level of trust in you that I have never known before. Help me, Lord, trust you with all my heart and not lean on my own understanding. I give myself back to you for that purpose, in Jesus's name. Amen.

Meditation #10

FEAR NOT

Teach me your way, Lord, that I may rely on your faithfulness; give me an undivided heart, that I may fear your name (Psalm 86:11).

KEY THOUGHT

We are called to be one-kingdom people, which means cultivating a holy, reverent fear of God.

TEACHING

Psalm 86:11 carries great meaning for me. I first really focused on this verse while on a recent trip to Hong Kong. Early one morning while going through my e-mail I received a deeply disappointing piece of news. I was physically shaken. Knowing that I had several speaking engagements coming up (on the subject of trust in God, no less), I shut my laptop off, opened my scripture, and began to read and pray. It was during those moments that my eyes found this wonderful psalm, and it changed my heart, my attitude, and my mind-set. It set me free to finish the week well, and it continues to be a source of blessings and challenge.

There is so much in this short scripture that we will use it as a text for the next two devotions. For me, the centerpiece is found in the third phrase, "give me an undivided heart." I have found that this verse speaks most powerfully if it is read in reverse. The reason that I have a divided heart is because I don't really, fully fear God and God alone. So I start there and ask, "What does it mean to fear the name of God?"

There is an old saying that goes, "If you fear God, you will fear nothing else; if you do not fear God, you will fear everything else." I find that to be very true in my life. Over three hundred times in scripture we are told, "Fear not." So why do we still fear things like financial downturns, personnel challenges, an uncertain future, failure of strategy, loss of reputation, and more? To the extent that we fear these things, we live with a divided heart. This is the reason we see our organizations as our "second kingdom." We want to have control over those things we fear, believing that if we have the power over them, we can drive away the fear. Of course the opposite happens. The more we try to control, the more we realize how little control we have, which causes us to fear all the more.

The first question that arises from this text is simply this: What do you fear today? Fearing God does not mean terror or dread but being overwhelmed by His sovereignty, His awesomeness, and His authority over every area of life. Here's the irony: a proper fear of the Lord is our greatest comfort. It drove Paul to ask, "If God is for us, who can be against us?" (Romans 8:31).

What will it require for you to cultivate such a holy, reverent fear of God that all other fear will be driven from your life and leadership?

ACTION

Look at a Bible concordance (likely in a good Bible study app) and look up ten verses that have the phrase "fear not" in them. Meditate on them today and ask God to cultivate in your heart an awesome fear of Him that drives out all other fear.

Prayer

Awesome and holy God, I confess that I have too often made you very small in my life. If you were to give me a tiny glimpse for one brief moment of your true majesty, it would drive me to my knees in holy fear and humble worship. I do not fear who you are, because I know your heart. I know that you love me dearly, that I am precious in your sight. But I do not want to lose the sense of awe and wonder that comes from understanding your holiness. Cultivate in my heart a proper fear of you. Help me become so overwhelmed by your majesty that my heart has no place remaining for the fear of anything else. Set me free from all other fear by your amazing love. In your mighty and awesome name I pray, amen.

Meditation #11

LEADING WITH AN UNDIVIDED HEART

Teach me your way, Lord, that I may rely on your faithfulness; give me an undivided heart, that I may fear your name (Psalm 86:11).

KEY THOUGHT

We are called to be one-kingdom people, which means developing an undivided heart.

TEACHING

Yesterday we looked at this psalm and considered what it means to fear God only. Cultivating a holy, reverent fear of God immediately challenges my divided heart. If I truly fear God, the motivation to divide my heart between the kingdom of God and the things of this world is driven away from me.

The enemy was able to drive a wedge into the hearts of the first couple in the Garden of Eden. They were created with the awesome opportunity to love God and God only. It's unthinkable that they would do anything else. The great Swiss theologian Karl Barth described the fall as "the impossible possibility." Although it was possible, it was also incomprehensible. Yet the enemy succeeded by turning Eve's attention away from complete trust in God and to the prospect of placing her own needs and desires on the throne of her life. As she contemplated what it might be like to be like God, her heart became divided.

We reenact that sin every time our divided hearts convince us to play the lord of our lives and grab control for ourselves. Once the heart is divided, once we seek to have loyalty to two kingdoms with two different lords, we experience fear, stress, anxiety, and worry that were never intended to be in the heart of a child of God.

How do we reclaim an undivided heart? We can do so through worship—that is, a total surrender to the sovereign God and Creator of all things. It really comes back to a holy fear of God, that awesome, overwhelming understanding of God's ultimate control of all things. From that fear come trust, faith, and a deep-seated desire to walk according to His will in obedience and joy. When that kind of reverence and worship overwhelms us, it drives from our hearts every competing loyalty.

Where has your heart been divided?

ACTION

There is a saying in politics that if you want to know the real reason why someone speaks, acts, or votes in a certain way, "follow the money." I believe there is a parallel for leaders here in this lesson. If you want to figure out where in your life you have compromise, conformity, and disobedience, "follow the fear." What you fear will lead you back to what you love, what you worship, and in what (or in whom) you put your trust. The challenge in today's lesson is to follow your fears, your stresses, your worries, and your anxieties back to their source. When you arrive there, acknowledge your divided heart and pray that the fear of God and God alone may overwhelm you.

Prayer

Gracious and loving Lord, I confess to you today that I have a divided heart. I have allowed the things of this world to creep into my spirit as a leader, to become the object of my focus, the center of my attention, and the source of my fear. If I follow my fear, it leads me back to so many things in my role as a leader that I have not submitted to you. I don't know why I hold on so tightly when you offer me freedom. I deeply long for an undivided heart. I pray that you begin to work in me to help me reclaim such a heart, and let that work begin with a love and fear of you that drives out everything else from my spirit. Lord, give me an undivided heart. In Jesus's name, amen.

Meditation #12

RELIANCE ON GOD'S FAITHFULNESS

Teach me your way, Lord, that I may rely on your faithfulness; give me an undivided heart, that I may fear your name (Psalm 86:11).

KEY THOUGHT

We are called to be one-kingdom people, which means a total reliance on God's faithfulness.

TEACHING

This is our third day meditating on Psalm 86:11. I proposed that this psalm may best be read in reverse order, so we started with an understanding of what it meant to fear God and God alone. From there we looked at the undivided heart and how true fear of God can so overwhelm us that it can bring the heart back to its one rightful object of worship. We conclude by looking at the first two phrases.

The key word for me here is "reliance." You can suggest your own synonym: trust, dependence, counting on, having confidence in, being sure about, etc. All of them point to an uncompromised attitude toward the source of our reliance. What is even more assuring is that it is the faithfulness of God upon which we rely. It should be staggering to us to consider the idea of the almighty God being faithful to us. Actually, in being faithful to us, He is simply being faithful to himself—to His own nature as the steadfast lover of our souls.

So here is a progression. When we are overwhelmed by the fear of God, His sovereign majesty and amazing love and grace for us drive out any division in our hearts and focus us back solely and completely on Him. As our hearts are healed, we are able to lead in absolute confidence of the faithfulness of God. As leaders we rely day by day, moment by moment, on the unwavering presence, power, and transforming grace of the God who created us, redeemed us, and calls us back to himself in Jesus Christ.

All of this is ours as a part of the work of the faithful steward leader. This is a journey that requires a level of trust and obedience that is beyond ourselves. It is fraught with challenges we cannot overcome on our own. And it runs counter to the world in which we live, which means this journey always puts us at odds with the world. This is not the human way, the self-centered way, or the world's way of talking about "successful leadership." It is God's way. And for that reason, we need to pray every day, "Lord, teach us your way."

Upon what or whom are you depending today? How you answer that question will determine your leadership style, shape your heart, and define your fears. What would it mean for you to rely solely on the faithfulness of God? Will you pray today, "Lord, teach me your way"?

Action

Depending on God for everything can be a rather overwhelming task. So start small. Choose one thing in your work today that you believe you depend on more than you do God. It may be your skills, your team, your financial situation, your strategy, etc. Ask yourself, "Do I rely on this so much that I am fearful of losing it?" If so, let your focus today be on surrendering it back to God and asking that He show you His way. Your prayer should be for your reliance on God to replace every other reliance in your life. See if one day of focus brings you a sense of freedom and peace in that area of your life. If so, make this yielding process a part of your daily walk or other daily introspective time, and one by one, yield everything back to Him until you begin to experience the joy of the undivided heart of a steward leader.

Prayer

Loving and merciful heavenly Father, these days I seem to be relying on so many things other than your faithfulness. I have to admit it is overwhelming for me to think that you are faithful to me, when in so many ways in my life it seems I am unfaithful to you. But that is your promise, and I claim it today. Cultivating my heart, Lord, I feel a deep sense of reliance on you alone. I don't know how to do this, but you have encouraged me to pray that you show me your ways. My heart is open, my spirit is waiting, so Lord, teach me your ways that I may rely on your faithfulness. Give me an undivided heart that I may fear your name. In Jesus's name, amen.

Meditation #13

THE POWER OF TESTIMONY

Then the high priest and all his associates, who were members of the party of the Sadducees, were filled with jealousy. They arrested the apostles and put them in the public jail. But during the night an angel of the Lord opened the doors of the jail and brought them out. "Go, stand in the temple courts," he said, "and tell the people all about this new life." At daybreak they entered the temple courts, as they had been told, and began to teach the people. When the high priest and his associates arrived, they called together the Sanhedrin—the full assembly of the elders of Israel—and sent to the jail for the apostles. But on arriving at the jail, the officers did not find them there. So they went back and reported, "We found the jail securely locked, with the guards standing at the doors; but when we opened them, we found no one inside." On hearing this report, the captain of the temple guard and the chief priests were at a loss, wondering what this might lead to. Then someone came and said, "Look! The men you put in jail are standing in the temple courts teaching the people." At that, the captain went with his officers and brought the apostles. They did not use force, because they feared that the people would stone them (Acts 5:17–26).

KEY THOUGHT

When we step off the thrones of our second kingdom, we have been set free for one primary purpose: to be used by God to set others free.

Teaching

In this wonderful text, we learn something about the nature of freedom. Peter and the apostles are thrown in jail, enslaved because of their preaching. They know that their testimony about Jesus put their lives in danger. Being thrown in prison is clear evidence that their time might be running out. Then God does the miraculous and sets them free. At this point I would accept this miracle with gratitude and see this as an opportunity to keep quiet and get out of Dodge. After all, you can't keep expecting God to bail you out. Having been given my freedom and escaping a possible life prison sentence or even death, I would learn my lesson and slip away quietly into the night.

But that is not the effect of real freedom. Real freedom, God-given freedom, encourages and empowers the preaching of the word of God in a greater way than we ever thought possible. The timid leaders find courage in freedom. Apathetic leaders find passion in freedom. Leaders who are unsure of their abilities find confidence in freedom. And the result is an unquenchable drive to share this freedom with others. Peter and the apostles literally run back to the temple and, at the first rays of dawn, are testifying once again in the name of Jesus. Amazing.

You have not been set free to remain silent. You have been set free and placed in a position of leadership in order to be used by God to free others. That is an awesome truth. You cannot live as a faithful steward leader in a world enslaved by sin and keep your freedom to yourself. If you do, it is a counterfeit freedom, because real freedom, God-given freedom, must be shared.

Do you believe that it is God's will and purpose that every person in your organization, every human heart your work touches, and indeed every soul on the face of the earth be set free from sin and embrace the joy of the faithful steward as a follower of Jesus Christ? If so, how do you think God plans to accomplish so great a task? The answer is simple: He will do it through His people, through the army of steward-leader warriors that He will raise up and place in positions of authority throughout the world leading others to the freedom of the kingdom of God.

Who will God bring into your life today that still lives enslaved by the things that used to enslave you? What will you do with this newfound freedom? Will you humble yourself before God, open yourself to the empowering of the Holy Spirit, and be ready to be used by God as an agent of freedom in the lives of the people you lead and serve?

ACTION

I'm sure that somewhere in your life you have experienced the power of personal testimony. Someone stood up in church and shared a moving story about what God did in his or her life. Or perhaps a missionary spoke in your church about the miraculous deeds she saw God do in her work. There may be no more powerful form of communication than the testimony of a credible witness to an amazing feat of God. If you have truly been set free at some point along this journey, then you have just such a testimony. Your challenge is to write it down word for word. Don't worry about the length or even the quality of the narrative. Write from your heart. Share what it felt like when the chains fell, when you first sensed real freedom in an area where you have known only bondage for so long. Once you have finished it, share it with your spouse, your pastor, and a few close colleagues. Ask them to tell you what they felt as they read it. You will be amazed at the power of your story, even in the lives of those you might consider to be spiritual giants. My prayer is that this experience will encourage you to find ways to share it more broadly within your organization however the spirit might lead you. Remember, you have been set free in order to be used by God to set other people free. Your testimony to freedom as a steward leader is a great tool for that purpose.

Prayer

Gracious Lord, it is hard for me to imagine myself as one who boldly proclaims your word in the public square. I have a hard time admitting that I'm a Christian in certain circles of friends. But you have set me free. I cannot deny the work that the Holy Spirit has done in my heart during this journey. I am so thankful, so deeply grateful for this freedom. If you can use me in the process of helping our people know that same freedom, then I submit myself to you for that purpose. As I have stepped off my throne and surrendered everything back to you, help me develop a personal testimony about this experience and give me the courage to share it with others. I cannot hide this under a bushel. Give me that same zeal that you placed in the heart of Peter and the apostles that I too might emerge from my chains and in my freedom run with excitement to tell others. Oh Lord, give me such a passion. In the name of Christ who came to set us free, amen.

Meditation #14

THRONE OF GRACE

In him [Jesus Christ] and through faith in him, we may approach God with freedom and confidence (Ephesians 3:12).

KEY THOUGHT

As faithful stewards we can draw with confidence before the throne of grace.

TEACHING

I can't imagine a more fitting verse with which to this section than Ephesians 3:12. A companion verse is Hebrews 4:16: "Let us then approach God's throne of grace with confidence, so that we may receive mercy and find grace to help us in our time of need."

Both of these verses are a blessed assurance that we can know with certainty that our God loves us, is for us, and deeply desires a relationship with us. We have been set free in Christ, and that freedom includes the redemption of our relationship with God. The temple curtain has been split, and we can now approach the almighty God of the universe with total confidence.

These are the two marks of the steward leader: freedom and confidence. As we remember from the last meditation, we are involved in a significant spiritual battle. Therefore, we can acknowledge here that the enemy seeks to work bondage and doubt in us, which both lead to fear. Paul challenges: "It is for freedom that Christ has set us free. Stand firm, then, and do not let yourselves be burdened again by a yoke of slavery" (Galatians 5:1).

God gives us freedom in Christ, and the enemy works every day to enslave us again to the bondage of leading through ownership and control. God gives us confidence through the blood of Christ, and the enemy whispers in our ears every day, "Did God really say that?"

Here is where the battle lines are drawn. Experiencing God's freedom daily requires us to battle against all of the tactics of the enemy. That is the main purpose of this entire journey. It is to provide us with the keys to unlock the bonds we put on ourselves as leaders by listening to the wrong voices, believing the lies of the enemy, and conforming ourselves to the world. My prayer is that, one by one, these chains will fall from you and you will experience the full freedom that is yours as a steward leader and child of the King.

The same is true for the precious gift of confidence. When our confidence in every area of our lives is found solely in the sovereignty, grace, and love of our triune God, we can be set free to lead. Confidence can only be developed in the context of an intimate relationship. We are confident in God because we know Him! But we must not take this for granted. The enemy wants to distract us and keep us focused on anything but Christ, for he knows that when our gaze is fixed on our Lord, our Lord can and will do mighty things in us and through us as steward leaders.

Confidence and freedom, freedom and confidence. This is your legacy as a steward leader.

Action

This action step is simple. Take a small piece of paper and write these two words on it: "confidence" and "freedom." Spend this day meditating on those two words. Pray that the Spirit opens your eyes to see those places in your life where doubt and bondage have crept in. Claim these words for yourself. Thank God for these gifts. Pray for protection from the enemy in these areas of your life. Rejoice, celebrate, and be glad that the God who created you for a relationship with himself wants to set you free to lead with a deep-seated confidence that you are His beloved child forever.

Prayer

Almighty, everlasting God, I thank you for these two wonderful words: "confidence" and "freedom." So often my leadership has reflected uncertainty and bondage. Instill in me the confidence that comes from your love for me and the purpose for which you created me. And let me know the freedom that is mine through your Son, Jesus Christ. You created me to live with this confidence and freedom. I claim them both today, not by my own power but through the power of the Holy Spirit. Thank you for these wonderful gifts. Let me be a faithful steward leader as I open myself up to you and let you work in and through me so that I may be your witness to my organization and the world. In Jesus's name, amen.

Part III

FROM STAGNANCY TO INTIMACY: THE HEART OF THE STEWARD LEADER

Steward leaders believe that everything in all of life belongs to God. Everything. That includes our relationship with God himself. How do we "steward" our relationship with God? This is an especially critical question for leaders. Our roles are so demanding of our time and attention that it is easy to let our time with God slip away. Faithful Christian leadership requires intimacy with God. This is the heart of a steward leader. Our relationship with God is the bedrock of our leadership, and so we steward the precious gift of intimacy that God offers us in Jesus Christ by the power of the Spirit.

This Trinitarian intimacy is the unremitting target of the enemy. And his greatest weapon is business. He delights in deceiving us into becoming so involved in our work for God that we squeeze out all opportunities for God to work in us. His goal is our spiritual stagnancy that comes when we seek to accomplish things for Jesus and stop seeking Jesus himself.

I pray these next seven meditations will give you opportunities to look for that stagnancy in your life, and to develop some discipline that can reorient you toward a deeper intimacy with Christ. This is not just a good thing to do; our veracity and faithfulness as leaders depend on it.

Meditation #15

ARE YOU CONVINCED?

As the Father has loved me, so have I loved you. Now remain in my love. If you keep my commands, you will remain in my love, just as I have kept my Father's commands and remain in his love. I have told you this so that my joy may be in you and your joy may be complete (John 15:9).

Key Thought

If you want to experience the abundant, joyful, and fulfilling life in Jesus Christ, it's all about location.

Teaching

Sometimes in scripture Jesus makes a comment that causes me to scrunch up my forehead or raise my eyebrows. John 15:9 is one of those verses. The statement is simple: "remain in his love." But have you ever wondered just what Jesus was talking about? To remain is to stay in a place. The opposite of remain is leave, go away, or remove yourself. As strange as it may sound, a fulfilling life in Christ is all about location.

We may be tempted to ask, "Isn't God's love everywhere?" Is there really a certain location where we are to go and sit and wait to experience this love? Well, I believe the answer is no and yes. We can answer no if we are looking for some physical place, like a church, a mountaintop, or a quiet lakeside, where we must go to know the love of God. However, we must answer yes if we are looking for a place to which God calls us and expects us to meet Him and experience His love. Simply put, it is in the presence of God that we experience the love of God. Jesus is calling us to remain in Him, knowing that it is in Him and Him alone that we will experience the overwhelming presence of His eternal and unconditional love for us.

This might lead us to ask, "Where else would we be if not in God's presence?" I must be clear that I am talking about our location, not God's. He never leaves us, but we can certainly isolate ourselves from His presence in our lives. And where might we go? Well, the enemy is happy to provide us with lots of beautiful, glossy travel brochures inviting us to journey to all kinds of places that will take us away from the presence of God. Consider some of the following alternate locations. When we live with unrepentant sin in our lives, we feel as if God is a thousand miles away. When, in our pride, we lead in selfishness, we lose a sense of intimacy with God. When we allow fear and anxiety to overwhelm us, we get the sense that we are all alone. When the cares of our leadership work steal from us all sense of hope, we live in despair.

The reality of each of these locations is that it is we who have moved and not God. Regardless of how far we run, how diligently we hide, how forcefully we rebel, the presence and love of God in Jesus Christ is as close as our very breath. All we need to do is turn our face toward Him with a simple prayer: "Lord, I want to remain in your love." As leaders we need that reassurance every day. So this is an invitation to draw near to God and experience afresh the love of Jesus Christ for you and to meditate on this verse:

For I am convinced that neither death nor life, neither angels nor demons, neither the present nor the future, nor any powers, neither height nor depth, nor anything else in all creation will be able to separate us from the love of God that is in Christ Jesus our Lord (Romans 8:38).

Are you convinced? Then remain in His love!

ACTION

There are countless reasons why you may not be experiencing today the love that God has for you. The most important leadership action you can take today is to set aside all the distractions in your life and meditate on this one thought: "God loves me unconditionally, lavishly, and eternally." Let that reality overwhelm you. Don't let anything today distract you from the certainty of this great truth. Say it to yourself over and over again until it seeps deeply into your spirit. If you open up your heart and allow God's Spirit to work in you today, regardless of where you are in your faith, you will experience the transformational love of God in a new and powerful way. All you need to do is ask.

May your unfailing love come to me, Lord—your salvation, according to your promise (Psalm 119:41).

PRAYER

Gracious and loving God, you invite me to remain in your love. I am here, open, waiting expecting, and yearning to know your love for me in a new and deeper way. You promised me that if I would draw closer to you, you would respond. I am here, Lord. I know that you love me, but I pray today that you would help me experience that love in a way that brings comfort, assurance, and peace. There are things in my life that make it feel like I have been separated from your love. I confess to you now that it is I who have moved and not you. And so, Lord, I am coming back. I may not know how, nor do I have the power to overcome those things continually drawing me away from you. So

I come to you humbly, in need, and with a passionate desire to remain in your love. I love you, Lord—let me experience afresh your love for me. I pray this in the name of the one who, for the joy of this moment, endured the cross for me, Jesus Christ, my Lord. Amen.

Meditation #16

HAVE YOU DIED?

And he [Jesus] said, "The Son of Man must suffer many things and be rejected by the elders, the chief priests and the teachers of the law, and he must be killed and on the third day be raised to life." Then he said to them all: "Whoever wants to be my disciple must deny themselves and take up their cross daily and follow me. For whoever wants to save their life will lose it, but whoever loses their life for me will save it" (Luke 19:22–24).

KEY THOUGHT

The world tells us that happiness comes from self-indulgence. Scripture tells us that satisfaction and joy come from self-denial. Even more radical, the true, abundant life we were created to live starts with death.

TEACHING

It's ironic that the verse that may promise the greatest level of joy in life is the one we like to hide away and talk about the least. You seldom see a church marquee announcing that "Deny Yourself! Take Up Your Cross and Follow Me" is the title for next Sunday's sermon. Few altar calls announce this condition as part of the decision to follow Christ. This is not a "seeker-friendly" scripture. Yet it is the heart and soul of the Gospel. Why do I make such a claim?

Our hearts can only know one ruler. Our lives can only

follow one leader. Our passions can only focus on one object. Our allegiance can only fall to one Lord. Our choice to follow one ruler means absolute rejection of all alternatives. The object of our love requires us to forsake all others. It's not who you are leading, but who is leading you that matters!

Commitment to one path and one leader means leaving every other possible route behind. Committing our life in one direction means absolute death to all other competing possibilities. I know we wish this weren't so. We wish we could keep our options open, play the field, and explore all possibilities without closing the door on any of them. But in our spiritual lives, a vacillating loyalty is a choice for self-indulgence over the walk of faith.

What is at stake in this decision is the gift of true intimacy with God. It is only when we deny all of the selfish alternatives that we find the life that is lived in the presence and bright countenance of the God who created us for himself. If we want to know the joy of that life, we have to lose all other, counterfeit alternatives. In essence, we have to die to the life that is focused on the self. And out of this death comes freedom, certainty, and the peace of God that passes all understanding.

This amazing life awaits us all on the other side of death— not our physical death but the death we are called to die every morning. It is a glorious death, and once we experience it we will thirst for it again and again. For as we die, we bury along with this old, false self its fears, anxieties, worries, and despairs. It is critical that we, as steward leaders, are willing to die this death! For as we do, we enter into an intimacy with God we will know only on the far side of this joyful death.

Have you died today?

Set your minds on things above, not on earthly things. For you died, and your life is now hidden with Christ in God. When

Christ, who is your life, appears, then you also will appear with Him in glory (Colossians 3:2–4).

ACTION

Write Colossians 3:2–4 on a 3" ′ 5" card. Put it someplace where you will see it first thing every morning: next to your alarm clock, taped to the dashboard of your car, or on your desk. Then make a commitment every morning to consider what it will mean for you that day to claim this death for yourself that you may truly live for Christ.

PRAYER

Gracious Lord, I confess to you that I have lived too much of my life for myself. As long as I live for myself, I can never experience the kind of intimacy and relationship that you wish for me. I'm tired of going it alone. I have to be honest—this kind of death to self scares me. There's so much of myself I want to hold on to, to trust in, and to rely upon. So help me, Lord, through the power of your Holy Spirit, to completely let go and die to myself. There's so much in this life that you have for me, and I will never experience it or know it until I know you fully. So take my life, Lord—I give it to you fully and completely. I name and set aside all those things in my life that are screaming at me for my allegiance. I am ready to lose my life—this old, painful, fear-filled, and anxious life. And I am ready to find the new life you have for me in Jesus Christ. Take my life, Lord, as it is yours. In Jesus's name, amen.

Meditation #17

DEFINING SUCCESS

Then he said to them, "Watch out! Be on your guard against all kinds of greed; life does not consist in an abundance of possessions" (Luke 12:15).

KEY THOUGHT

How you measure success in this life will dictate the way you live this life and the legacy you will leave.

TEACHING

In my work as a consultant for not-for-profit organizations, I ask one question to start almost every consultation: "How do you measure success?" I have found that this question more than any other helps define an organization's mission, values, and motivations. The same is true for us as leaders. Each of us carries with us a definition of success for your life and leadership. That definition impacts our attitudes, our actions, and every decision we make.

Chuck Colson, the founder of Prison Fellowship, had a plaque on his desk for most of the years he ran the ministry. It read, "Not Success but Faithfulness." It was a daily reminder to him that success in the kingdom of God was radically different than in the world. In fact, the idea of success itself had to be replaced by a radically new idea, the call to absolute faithfulness for followers of Jesus Christ. The great challenge for us as leaders is that so often faithfulness as a follower of Jesus Christ will result in things that run absolutely counter to the world's definition of leadership success. Scripture absolutely promises this. It tells us that in the kingdom of God we live by dying, receive by giving, lead by serving, become first by being last, and are exalted through humility.

It is, however, even more radical than that. Success defined in kingdom terms can be boiled down to this one simple definition: a life lived daily in an intimate relationship with God through Jesus Christ, in the power of the Holy Spirit. It is in this intimacy that our hearts are changed and our lives transformed, and faithfulness becomes our driving motivation in every area of our lives.

Without this intimacy we see counterfeit definitions of success as a leader. Our culture screams at us that success has to do with how fast we grow our organization, how much money we can raise or earn, the amount of power we wield, and the reputation we cultivate. These aberrant definitions seep their way into the kingdom of God and deceive leaders who try to weave them into their work. But they are antithetical to the way of the cross.

Are you willing to embrace kingdom values to such an extent that you will measure the success of your leadership solely and completely in terms of your faithfulness as a follower of Jesus, which is born from an intimate relationship with God? When Jesus proclaims in John 10, "I have come that you may have life and have it abundantly," he is referring to this life of faithfulness. It is the life of a steward leader. Are you living the abundant life of a steward leader today? It starts with an intimate relationship with God in Jesus Christ and a heart that yearns for faithfulness as the driving force behind everything you think, say, and do.

Action

Write your own one- to two-sentence definition for success. Consider the mental picture this definition creates, the image you hold of the ideal place you want to be in life. All of us are striving toward some picture of a life that is beyond the one we are living today. How well does it align with the definition of success as absolute faithfulness as a steward leader? Are you willing to identify those driving forces in your life that do not align with Kingdom values? Pray about each one, asking that God would change your heart, as you grow deeper in your relationship with Him. Let that become your heart's desire.

Prayer

Gracious Lord, I confess that I have focused my attention on attaining things in this life that look a lot like the world's definition of success. It is so easy for me to desire financial security, a glowing reputation, popularity, praise, and even power in my leadership role. I admit that in pursuing these things, I have lost my way. I am not experiencing the abundant life you promised me. Take me back into your presence and help me find true intimacy with you. In your presence, change my heart, open my eyes, and give me a new vision for my leadership. Instill in me a passion for faithfulness that will overwhelm every other passion in my life. I want to follow you, and you alone, with all my heart. Come, Holy Spirit, and guide me into all truth. I give myself back to you for this purpose in the name of my Lord and Savior Jesus Christ. Amen.

Meditation #18

FRUIT THAT LASTS

But seek first his kingdom and his righteousness, and all these things will be given to you as well (Matthew 6:33).

I am the true vine, and my Father is the gardener. He cuts off every branch in me that bears no fruit, while every branch that does bear fruit he prunes so that it will be even more fruitful. You are already clean because of the word I have spoken to you. Remain in me, as I also remain in you. No branch can bear fruit by itself; it must remain in the vine. Neither can you bear fruit unless you remain in me. I am the vine; you are the branches. If you remain in me and I in you, you will bear much fruit; apart from me you can do nothing (John 15:1–5).

KEY THOUGHT

We can become so busy trying to change the world for Christ that we have no time for Christ to change us.

TEACHING

A number of years ago, God confronted me with a significant fallacy that I had been living with for most of my adult life. It had to do with John 15. I had always considered this text to be a charge to be producers of fruit as followers of Jesus. To me this meant setting and achieving goals, seeing tangible results for our work, and making an impact on the kingdom of God. It threw me into a lifestyle of incessant busyness—all for Jesus, of course.

Then one day he laid on my heart the realization that John 15 may not be about producing fruit at all. Again and again Jesus uses the term "bearing," and there is a significant difference between producing and bearing fruit. The former focuses on my work for God, the latter on God's work through me. John 15 is less a call to action than an invitation to intimacy. Eleven times Jesus uses the term "remain." There is an undeniable link between remaining in an intimate relationship with God and the extent to which our lives will bear this fruit.

There is one more piece to this puzzle. It is in how we define "fruit." If the fruit in our life is always defined as the product of our labor, the work of our hands, the outcome of our own efforts, then we will completely miss the message of John 15. Consider instead that what Jesus is talking about as fruit, the apostle Paul later defined for us as the "fruit of the Spirit" in Galatians 5. This shift in definition was one of the most shocking discoveries of my Christian life. Instead of demanding of me the driven life of trying to do good things for God, Jesus is inviting me into a relationship with Him that is so deep, so intimate, that my life will be filled with the Holy Spirit. As that Spirit works in and through me, my life will bear love, joy, peace, patience, kindness, goodness, gentleness, faithfulness, and self-control.

The impact of this fruit on the people we lead will result from what God is doing in us and through us and not just from what we are doing for Him. In fact, our drivenness for doing may be the single greatest obstacle to the Spirit's work in us as leaders. We can become so busy working for God that we lose the depth of relationship with Him that is required for Him to work in us. When our work becomes our fruit, it carries no power to change or transform.

What kind of fruit is being produced in your life and

leadership? Are you so busy trying to do what God wants you to do that you have lost the depth of relationship with Him that will allow Him to live in and through you? To what extent is the fruit of the Spirit being poured out through your leadership into the lives of the people you lead and serve?

Action

Send an e-mail to three people who know you well. List in your e-mail the fruits of the Spirit from Galatians 5 and ask them to what extent they see this fruit being borne out in your life. Be open to their response to let it guide you in seeking deeper intimacy with God from which this fruit will grow.

Prayer

Gracious Lord, I confess to you that I can too easily focus on the work I am doing for you at the expense of letting you work in me and through me. You know, Lord, that I want to be fruitful for the kingdom. Forgive me if I have misunderstood what that means. I look at my life as a leader and wonder to what extent the fruit of the Spirit is being experienced by people whose lives I touch each day. Sometimes I see that in my drive to produce fruit for you, I have actually taken on attitudes and actions that are in complete contradiction to this fruit. Please forgive me. I deeply desire a more intimate relationship with you. Please change my heart and attitudes and help me become a fruit bearer for the kingdom of God. I want the Holy Spirit to flow through me, but I'm not sure how to get there. So come, Holy Spirit, overwhelm my spirit and create in me a fresh and clean heart. I yield myself back to you for this purpose. In Jesus's name, amen.

Meditation #19

THE MYTH OF GODLY DRIVENNESS

What do people get for all the toil and anxious striving with which they labor under the sun? All their days their work is grief and pain; even at night their minds do not rest. This too is meaningless. A person can do nothing better than to eat and drink and find satisfaction in their own toil. This too, I see, is from the hand of God, for without him, who can eat or find enjoyment? To the person who pleases him, God gives wisdom, knowledge, and happiness, but to the sinner he gives the task of gathering and storing up wealth to hand it over to the one who pleases God. This too is meaningless, a chasing after the wind (Ecclesiastes 2:22–26).

KEY THOUGHT

God will not call you to a job or work that requires you to lead an unbalanced and unhealthy life in order to be successful.

TEACHING

We are all familiar with the logic formula "If A is true and B is true, then C must be true." Using that formula, let me share with you an A, B, and C that may prove disturbing to many of us.

A. God created us to live balanced and healthy lives. This includes time for work, time for family, time for fellowship and community, time for worship, time for rest, and time for devotion. Our lives reflect God's intention when each of these areas is given proper attention.

B. God created us for work. He calls us into leadership roles that use our skills and allow us to serve Him in whatever work we do. Whatever the job, it is a gift from God, and He intends us to employ our skills with excellence in carrying it out.

C. If God created us to live balanced and healthy lives (A), and if He created us for work that is meaningful and productive (B), then we must conclude (C) that God would never call us into a job or vocation that required us to sacrifice a healthy and balanced life in order for us to be successful.

How many of us are working sixty-plus-hour weeks, sacrificing marriage, family, and devotional time, believing that this amount of work is necessary to be successful leaders in the work God called us to do? Do you see the illogic of it? But worse, do you see the inherent evil that is being unleashed by a misunderstanding of God's intent?

How many marriages are being broken by one spouse's breakneck schedule? How many parent-child relationships are damaged by a parent who is never around, distracted by a "leadership calling" believed to be from God? How many men and women in leadership have moral failings due to a dryness of spirit that resulted from a work schedule that squeezed out every available moment for activities that built their reputations and left nothing that refreshed their souls?

It is a sin to be so driven. And it is a more grievous sin to believe that our drivenness is somehow the will of God. It is, in fact, a tool of the enemy to rob us of the life God created us to live. Why do we succumb to such a delusion? I believe it is a result of pride and fear. In our pride we believe that somehow God needs us, our organization needs us, our employees need us, the kingdom of God needs us. So we oblige by pouring ourselves into our work lest the world come to a halt if we do anything less. Or we operate out of a fear that if we slow down, we will fall behind. Everyone around us, including our pastor and other mentors, all seem to be on the same frenetic schedule. If we slow down, the world will pass us by, and we will miss out on all of the "rewards" of this stressful existence.

Whether through pride or fear, we are doing ourselves to death. If the logic formula is true, then we must conclude that whatever work God calls us to do, and whatever leadership role He has called us to assume, He does so with the expectation that we can carry out that work with excellence within a time commitment that will not detract from a balanced and healthy life. If our life is out of balance and our relationships are becoming unhealthy as a result, we are not doing God's will, no matter how much fruit we seem to be producing for the kingdom of God. That is a sobering reality for many, perhaps most, of us.

Will you examine your life according to this A, B, C formula? Will you acknowledge the sin that may be lurking in your drivenness to succeed?

Action

Sit with your spouse or close friend and define what a balanced and healthy life would look like. Identify the time commitments you would you need to make to each area to achieve this vision. Then ask God to give you a vision for a new approach to your work that aligns with His intent for you to live in healthy relationships and know the balance of life for which He created you.

Prayer

Gracious Lord, I confess to you that my life is not in balance. There never seems to be enough time in the day to do all the things that I believe you want me to do. Sometimes my devotional time gets sacrificed. Sometimes it's the time with my family, my spouse, or my friends. Too often I feel stressed and frustrated that I'm not able to get more done. My schedule is jammed, yet there's always more that I feel like I should be doing. I pray, Lord, that you would set me free from this cycle. Help me name those things that are important to the kind of healthy and balanced life for which you created me. Help me name what is driving my schedule, and through the power of your Holy Spirit, help me change. I want health in my life. I want balance in my life. And I know that's what you want for me. So I give myself back to you for whatever work you need to do for me to achieve this. In the name of the one who came to set us free, Jesus Christ, my Lord, amen.

✦

Meditation #20

THE ONE THING

As Jesus and his disciples were on their way, he came to a village where a woman named Martha opened her home to him. She had a sister called Mary, who sat at the Lord's feet listening to what he said. But Martha was distracted by all the preparations that had to be made. She came to him and asked, "Lord, don't you care that my sister has left me to do the work by myself? Tell her to help me!"

"Martha, Martha," the Lord answered, "you are worried and upset about many things, but few things are needed—or indeed only one. Mary has chosen what is better, and it will not be taken away from her" (Luke 10:38–42).

But whatever were gains to me I now consider loss for the sake of Christ. What is more, I consider everything a loss because of the surpassing worth of knowing Christ Jesus my Lord, for whose sake I have lost all things. I consider them garbage, that I may gain Christ and be found in him, not having a righteousness of my own that comes from the law, but that which is through faith in Christ—the righteousness that comes from God on the basis of faith (Philippians 3:7–9).

KEY THOUGHT

Can the purpose of life be boiled down to just one thing? Yes.

TEACHING

Both Mary and Paul know something quite extraordinary, life changing, and earth shaking. Of Mary, Jesus makes the remarkable claim that she discovered the one thing that is needed. Martha can't see it. She is distracted by things she considers to be extremely important. They upset her and worry her, causing her to become frantic and irritated.

Paul, on the other hand, seems to have lost touch with reality in his letter. Having built a great career with significant accomplishments, Paul equates everything he has done to a pile of cow dung. All because of this one thing that he tells us he has found. Has Paul gone mad?

It's likely all of us have sympathy for Martha, having been left alone to prepare the meal for Jesus and His entourage. Mary sits at Jesus's feet and listens to Him while her sister runs around. Is this really a commendable choice? After all, if we all chose to be Mary, nothing would get done! And what of Paul? Is it right to treat with disdain a lifetime of hard work, education, responsible labor, achievements, accomplishments, and productivity? Isn't that unnecessarily extreme?

The reason for such a radical teaching as we find with both Mary and Paul reflects the power of the temptation in our lives to compromise when it comes to this one thing that is needed. Everything in our life, everything, flows from this one thing, this first thing, this all-important and all-encompassing thing. Knowing Jesus Christ as our Lord will be, in the end, all that really matters in life. Everything else we think, say, and do will reflect the level of this knowing. Therefore, knowing must have our first, primary, and unequivocal allegiance. Jesus tells us that if we will seek Him, and the kingdom of God, above all else, all the other things that would otherwise distract us will be taken care of. Do you believe that?

In an African American church I visited, the congregants had framed a saying and hung it in the entryway. It read, "The Main Thing Is to Keep the Main Thing the Main Thing."

Is the main thing in your life an unquenchable thirst and an unbridled drive to know Jesus Christ intimately and personally? That is the one thing that is needed. As leaders we must not miss this! If we do, we cannot be the leaders God has called us to be. We will miss the opportunity to lead as a steward and everything else in the life God created us to live. If, however, this is our priority, and we seek it with our whole heart, then we can trust in His promise that everything else will be taken care of by His loving hand.

Action

Record this saying someplace where you can see it on a daily basis: "The main thing is to keep the main thing the main thing." This simple reminder can hold your eyes focused on Christ, your heart attuned to listening for His voice, and your hands employed in the work He called you to do for His glory.

Prayer

Gracious Lord, I confess that you are not always the main thing in my life. So often I feel like Martha, running around with my hectic schedule, my frenetic pace, trying to get so much done and wondering if it all really matters. And here you are, telling me that what is most important are the quiet times that I sit at your feet and listen to you. You remind me through Paul that everything else I try to do to gain recognition in this life pales in comparison to the time that I spend knowing you more deeply and intimately. Give me a heart that desires this intimacy. Give me courage to set aside the distractions of leadership that worry and upset me. Help me make the main thing the main thing in my life: knowing you and living daily in sweet communion with you. In Jesus's name, amen.

Meditation #21

PRAYER AS MEANS AND END

And when they found him on the other side of the sea, they said to him, "Rabbi, when did you come here?" Jesus answered them and said, "Most assuredly, I say to you, you seek me, not because you saw the signs, but because you ate of the loaves and were filled. Do not labor for the food which perishes but for the food which endures to everlasting life, which the Son of man will give you, because God the Father has set his seal on him." Then they said to him, "What shall we do, that we may work the works of God?" Jesus answered and said to them, "This is the work of God, that you believe in him whom he sent" (John 6:25–29).

KEY THOUGHT

We follow Jesus because of who He is and what He has already done for us, not because of what we want Him to do for us.

TEACHING

Why do you follow Jesus? Be careful, because the first answer you're likely to give may come more from what you were taught to say or what you'd like to be able to say rather than the truth that is in your heart. I know that's a tough statement, but I have recently had to struggle myself with how I answer that question. In the text above, Jesus challenges His followers to examine their hearts and see why they were pursuing Him so.

The first challenge in this text is Jesus's admonition that

people are only following Him because when they are hungry, He feeds them. In this way Jesus becomes a means to their own ends. If we hang around Jesus long enough, surely He'll have mercy on us, perform another clever miracle, and we'll all get a great meal. The same can be said for those who came to Him to be healed. They were interested in what Jesus could do for them, what need He could meet or what malady He could cure. They came because of what Jesus did, not because of who He was.

Do we struggle with the same thing today? Do we follow Jesus because of what He is able to do for us in our role as leaders? Do our prayers reflect our love for Him or our thirst for what we need Him to do for us?

There is a second challenge hidden in this tough text. At the end the disciples ask Jesus what they have to do in order to accomplish God's work on earth. In their desire to do the works of God, they ask Jesus for a checklist—a to-do list, if you will—that they can tick off to satisfy themselves that they are doing God's work. Here the focus shifts from what Jesus can do for us to what we can do for Jesus. His response should shock and challenge all of us who lead from a Protestant work ethic that is driving us to work ourselves into the grave. He says simply, "Believe in Him who He sent." That's it. The greatest work we will ever do for the sake of the kingdom of God is to believe, really believe with our whole heart, in who Jesus Christ is.

If this is true, we need to ask ourselves, how much of our time as leaders do we spend focusing on those things that we can check off a list, and how much time do we spend growing more intimately in love with God and growing our faith in the one He sent?

Both lessons remind us that God is more concerned with who we are (and who we are becoming in Him) than in what we do. He wants us to love Him for who He is and respond with a deep, growing, and abiding faith and trust in Him. If those priorities do not make their way to the top of our leadership goals and ambitions, we will miss the greatest gift ever given to humanity.

ACTION

Your one action step is to consider your prayer life. To what extent has God become the means to your own ends? Do you love Him, serve Him, and follow Him because of who He is, or has a self-serving spirit found its way into your prayer life? Do we love and follow Jesus because of all the mighty things He does or because of who He is? Lay this before God and ask for Him to help you regain the right attitude in your life of intimacy with Christ and prayer.

PRAYER

Gracious Lord, this is a really challenging text. Forgive me for the self-serving attitude that seems to creep into my prayer life from time to time. I get so focused on all of my responsibilities as a leader that I lose track of the importance and the sheer joy of being in your presence and worshiping you for the incredible God you are. Where I have lost intimacy with you, restore my passion to be in your presence and to love you for who you are. Let my prayers reflect my passion to worship you and let my requests be laid at your feet in humility and gratitude. And Lord, keep me from becoming so driven by all the things I think you want me to accomplish that I lose sight of this one powerful truth: you want me to believe and trust in you above all things. I do believe, Lord—help my unbelief. In the name of Jesus Christ, whom I love and serve, amen.

Part IV

From Distraction to Balance: The Image of the Steward Leader

Pride and discouragement: these are the distractions that can pull a leader off the straight path that leads to Jesus. Like Peter on the water, steward leaders must keep their eyes focused on Jesus, which means keeping their identity tied solely to Him. He is the source of our true self, the person God created us to be. He is the author of your image and the caretaker of your reputation. As long as we fix our gaze on Him and seek our affirmation from His grace and love, we can lead in freedom and joy.

The enemy holds out the two alternatives and tempts us to veer from this path and distract our gaze from Jesus as the source our identity. He uses pride to pull our dependence away from God and onto our self—our own abilities, skills, talents, and experience. As we do, our source of affirmation and identity shifts from God to man. We will seek human applause and thirst for the plaudits of our peers. When we let pride distract us, the road we travel will be strewn with broken relationships, dashed hopes, and disillusioned followers.

The same is true for the path of discouragement. When we lose faith, we again shift our focus from Christ, through whom we can do all things, and fix them on our disappointments, our wants, and our failures. Our identities become enmeshed with our failure, and we again have lost our way as leaders.

The freedom and joy of the steward leader is found in the center of the road, with our eyes fixed squarely on Jesus and our identities found solely in His affirmation of us as His called and chosen people. I pray the next seven meditations will help you either regain an identity you may have lost or help further strengthen the image you bear as a holy, righteous, beloved, redeemed child of God.

Meditation #22

THE LEADER IN THE MIRROR

The word of the Lord came to me, saying, "Before I formed you in the womb, I knew you; before you were born, I set you apart; I appointed you as a prophet to the nations" (Jeremiah 1:4–5).

For you created my inmost being; you knit me together in my mother's womb. I praise you because I am fearfully and wonderfully made; your works are wonderful, I know that full well. My frame was not hidden from you when I was made in the secret place, when I was woven together in the depths of the earth (Psalm 139:13–15).

KEY THOUGHT

God created you in His image and for His glory. Your identity lies solely in Him.

TEACHING

Three people were discussing the beginning of life. The first said confidently, "Life begins at conception." The second disagreed, arguing back, "No, life begins at viability." The third was old and gray. He listened intently and then exclaimed, "You're both wrong. Life begins when the last kid goes to college and the dog dies."

In the debates over abortion, stem cell research, genetic engineering, and embryonic cloning, the central, driving question addresses the moment that life begins. In essence, the answer to that is the very definition of life itself. While we, on the human, moral level, argue over this issue using science, philosophy, theology, and ethics, in the heart of God, the matter is clear and settled.

You were known by God before you were born, before you were conceived, before the very creation of the world. If God is the author and sustainer of life, then in a very real sense your life began when you were known by God before He uttered the words, "Let there be light." That's a pretty awesome thought!

God's first words to the prophet Jeremiah were meant to seal in his heart the nature of his temporal calling. "Before I formed you in the womb, I knew you." This text forces us to presume something incredibly audacious. God's eternal decision to create a world outside of himself included His decision that you and I would one day live in this world. The two are integrally connected. Our birth is no accident. And neither is our life, our purpose for being here, or God's intent to lead us into the life He created us to live. From God's knowing us before creation to His work of knitting us together from conception to birth, to His daily sustaining of us with life, breath, health, and all we need to live in this world, our life in its entirety belongs to Him. He chose the day of our birth, and He will choose the day that He takes us home. In between, every second is a gift from Him to be invested with joy in a relationship with Him; a relationship that includes loving ourselves, loving our neighbor, and loving this world that He created for us.

Every atom in your body belongs to Him; you are here solely because He willed you to be. How then can you possibly find your identity in any other source than this creating, sustaining, and loving God? We are children of God—that is our only possible identity as we walk this earth. And the spirit He put within us yearns every day to be reconnected with its Creator. As St. Augustine stated so eloquently, "Oh Lord, you created us for you, and our heart is restless until it finds its rest in you."*

ACTION

This may sound silly, but please take it seriously. Stand in front of a mirror and take a really good long look at yourself. Look into your eyes and say these words aloud so your ears can hear you say: "You are here for a purpose. You are part of God's plan from eternity. He could have chosen to create this world without you. But He didn't. He chose you. He chose your gender, He chose your skin color, He chose your height, He chose the color of your eyes and the size of your ears. He chose your smile, your gait, and the sound of your voice. He created you exactly as He intended. You are the product of His workmanship. You belong to Him. Your true identity is a child of God."

How does it feel to tell yourself this truth?

PRAYER

My dear, loving, and Creator God, it is hard for me to believe that you thought of me before the creation of the world. I am amazed that you planned for me to be here from the beginning of time. Despite my role as a leader, I often don't feel very important. I often feel unappreciated, undervalued, even useless. Help me, Lord, to live in this truth that I am your child, created for meaning and purpose in the life you prepared me to live. Drive out of my heart and mind all thoughts that pull me away from my sole identity in you. I give you back every day that you give me life and breath to walk this earth. Let my life be a joyful witness to you, my loving Creator, redeemer, sustainer, and friend. In Jesus's name, amen.

---

* Augustine, *The Confessions of St. Augustine*, trans. Edward Pusey (n.p.: Amazon Digital Services, 2012).

Meditation #23

WHO ARE YOU?

Then God said, "Let us make mankind in our image, in our likeness." So God made mankind in his own image, in the image of God he created them. Male and female, he created them (Genesis 1:27).

For those God foreknew he also predestined to be conformed to the image of his Son, that he might be the firstborn among many brothers and sisters (Romans 8:29).

For we are God's handiwork, created in Christ Jesus to do good works, which God prepared in advance for us to do (Ephesians 2:10).

Key Thought

God is more concerned with who we are, and who we are becoming in Him, than the work we produce each day.

Teaching

Imagine yourself at a social gathering. You bump into someone you have never met and politely introduce yourself. He responds by sharing his name, and then this person gives you an interesting command: "So, tell me who you are." You start to tell him what you do for a living, but he stops you and says, "No, don't tell me about your job—tell me who you are." A little confused, you begin to share with him that you are a parent, a spouse, a resident of the city in which you live, but he abruptly stops you again and demands, "No, don't tell me about the roles you play in life. I'm really interested to know who you are." Pretty unnerving, isn't it?

What is awkward when posed in a casual social situation is crucial to our definition of self. From our texts above we learn that our primary identity is as an image bearer of the God who created us. Since that original image was marred in the fall, and we have been redeemed in Jesus Christ, we are in the process of being shaped in His image. That too is our identity. From this sure and certain identity as a child of God being made in the image of Christ and the power of the Holy Spirit, we will live, act, and work in a certain way. Paul, in Ephesians, told us that the good works we do are part of God's greater plan.

The point I want to make here is that of direction. When we consider how to integrate who we are and what we do, scripture tells us there is only one acceptable direction. Our identity is in Christ, whose image we bear as a witness to the world. As we live out that identity, we will lead in ways that reflect that image. We can label this as a who-to-what direction. What we do is an outflow of who we are.

Here's the challenge. We live in a world that labels us and defines us more by what we do than who we are. We live in a what-to-who world. Tell me what you do, and I'll derive from it a level of value to your life. Even as followers of Jesus, we can fall into this trap all too easily. We can begin to find the definition of who we are in the roles we play, the titles we hold, and the outcomes we produce. This is especially true for leaders. We can allow the reputation of our organizations and the size of our budgets to define us. The world values power, prestige, possessions, and praise. People pursue these things with a passion, believing that in them they will find their identity as "successful" people.

But for a child of God, the process is exactly the opposite. If there is success to be had in this world, it comes solely from the extent to which we have submitted ourselves to Jesus Christ, allowing Him to live in us and through us. As that Spirit conforms our spirit to the image of Christ, then excellent, effective, and life-changing leadership flows from us. But that work never defines us. We are children of God, redeemed through Christ, and empowered by the Holy Spirit, period.

Action

Complete the following sentence, listing every title and role you play:

I am a(n)

_____, _____,
_____, _____,
_____, _____,
_____, _____,
_____, _____,
_____, _____,
_____, _____,
_____, _____,
_____, _____,
and _____.

Now think through this meditation, reread the texts, and answer the question posed by the guy at the party who asks, "Who are you?"

Prayer

Lord God, heavenly Father, I confess that as I read this I realized how often I have identified myself with what I do and not by who I am in you. It's so easy to be labeled by my job title, the influence I wield, and the esteem of others. I acknowledge that the world has pressed on me its values and too often I have accepted them as my own. Help me, through the power of your Holy Spirit, to reclaim my sole identity as a child of God being conformed to the image of Christ. I know that from this identity you can work through me to do good and great things in this world. I thank you for that. But never let me shift my identity to my work, or I will fall back into the same old trap that I'm already in. My identity is in you. Let me affirm that rich and wonderful truth every morning before my feet touch the floor. Help me live each day in the privilege and challenge of bearing your image in this broken and hurting world. In Jesus's name I pray, amen.

Meditation #24

NEITHER PRIDE NOR DOUBT

> *He and Aaron gathered the assembly together in front of the rock and Moses said to them, "Listen, you rebels, must we bring you water out of this rock?" Then Moses raised his arm and struck the rock twice with his staff. Water gushed out, and the community and their livestock drank. But the Lord said to Moses and Aaron, "Because you did not trust in me enough to honor me as holy in the sight of the Israelites, you will not bring this community into the land I give them"* (Numbers 20:10–12).

KEY THOUGHT

If we keep our eyes focused on Jesus Christ, and our identity secured in Him, we will resist the temptations of pride and self-doubt.

TEACHING

A few years ago, my wife and I traveled to Zion National Park. One of the hiking options was a climb up to Angels Landing, a tiny rock outcropping that soars above the canyon below, providing a breathtaking and terrifying view. Getting there is no picnic. After a long and winding trail, the last few hundred feet place you on a narrow path that has a chain rail on both sides—for good reason. As you grasp the chains and work your way along the path, you realize that on each side of you there is a fifteen-hundred-foot sheer drop. I realized that if I were to stop and look in either direction, vertigo would likely overtake me. So I fixed my eyes straight ahead on my destination and tried to ignore the gaping chasm that seem to call to me on both sides.

We have been focusing on what it means to find our sole identity in Jesus Christ. One way to picture it is as though you were standing in the middle of a path with both feet firmly on the ground, facing straight ahead and fixing your eyes on your destination. When you keep to the center of the path and don't become distracted, you can work your way through obstacles, around rocks, through streams, and up steep grades, all without losing your focus on your destination. When our eyes are focused on Jesus Christ as our sole identity, then all that the world can offer us will not cause us to veer from the path.

Yet we do veer. We must recognize that the enemy wants us anywhere but walking the center of this path. He continually places before us enticements to move off the path in one of two directions. If he can get our eyes off Jesus, he can woo us to the left where, in our pride, we believe we can really negotiate this path by ourselves. (We will consider the other option in the next meditation.) Pride always causes us to take our eyes off our goal and place it in some other desired location. Confident in ourselves and the strength of our leadership, we wander from the path and find ourselves soon out in the weeds (or, to return to my story above, we go over the cliff).

This desire to go it alone on his own strength motivated Moses to strike the rock. As a frustrated leader, he took matters into his own hands and provided his people what they wanted, water. Rather than trusting in God and seeking His will, Moses became the provider for his people—a role that belongs to God and God alone. Moses was hailed the savior and deliverer as the children of Israel drank fully from the water that flowed from the rock. But that was not Moses's calling or work.

Moses found himself off the path, having fixed his gaze someplace other than on his trust in God alone. And it cost Moses and the nation of Israel greatly. As leaders, when we grab control of the situations in our life—or become too great in our own eyes, seeking to provide for our own needs and chart our own path—we deny our identity in Christ and Christ alone. Like Moses, we may produce short-term results, but we cannot please God and live our lives according to His purpose.

Are you leading from a place that is squarely in the center of the path to which God has called you? Are your eyes fixed on Him every day? Or have you strayed off the path in your own pride and wandered from God's way due to your desire for control? Does your identity today rely on what you will do in your own power, or on who you are as a child of God?

Action

Think about your day yesterday. What was it that most controlled your decisions, your actions, your attitudes, your words, and your emotions? Was yesterday a day that you can say was lived with your eyes fully fixed on Jesus Christ and your feet walking a path directly to Him? If not, write down three things that you did yesterday that were symbolic of an overdependence on yourself or someone or something else. Once you have identified three things (decisions, actions, attitudes, words, emotions, etc.), acknowledge them before God and pray for the power to overcome the same temptations tomorrow. For they will be there waiting for you.

Prayer

Holy and almighty God, I confess that when I look back on my life I see so many places where I have strayed off the path to which you've called me. I don't know why, but sometimes I grab control as a leader and go in the direction I think is right. I take my eyes off you and focus on my own work. Other times I just get fearful, and out of my stress or anxiety, I wander off the path and try to go it alone. Even now, Lord, I don't find myself squarely in the middle of the road that leads to you. So bring me back, set my feet firmly on the right path, and fix my gaze on you. Help me walk to you today, step by step, moment by moment, decision by decision. Help me lead this day as a child of God, whose identity is in you alone. In Christ, my Savior and Redeemer, amen.

Meditation #25

FINDING OUR FEET

See, the Lord your God has given you the land. Go up and take possession of it as the Lord, the God of your ancestors, told you. Do not be afraid; do not be discouraged (Deuteronomy 1:21).

The Lord himself goes before you and will be with you; he will never leave you nor forsake you. Do not be afraid; do not be discouraged (Deuteronomy 31:8).

Be strong and courageous. Do not be afraid; do not be discouraged, for the Lord your God will be with you wherever you go (Joshua 1:9).

Then the Lord said to Joshua, "Do not be afraid; do not be discouraged. Take the whole army with you and go up and attack Ai. For I have delivered into your hands the king of Ai, his people, his city, and his land" (Joshua 8:1).

Joshua said to them, "Do not be afraid; do not be discouraged. Be strong and courageous. This is what the Lord will do to all the enemies you are going to fight" (Joshua 10:25).

Then you will have success if you are careful to observe the decrees and laws that the Lord gave Moses for Israel. Be strong and courageous. Do not be afraid or discouraged (1 Chronicles 22:13).

David also said to Solomon, his son, "Be strong and courageous and do the work. Do not be afraid or discouraged, for the Lord God, my God, is with you. He will not fail you or forsake you until all the work for the service of the temple of the Lord is finished" (1 Chronicles 28:20).

He said: "Listen, King Jehoshaphat and all who live in Judah and Jerusalem! This is what the Lord says to you: 'Do not be afraid or discouraged because of this vast army. For the battle is not yours, but God's'" (2 Chronicles 20:15).

You will not have to fight this battle. Take up your positions; stand firm, and see the deliverance the Lord will give you, Judah and Jerusalem. Do not be afraid; do not be discouraged. Go out to face them tomorrow, and the Lord will be with you (2 Chronicles 20:17).

Key Thought

God encourages the discouraged and humbles the proud in order to keep us in the center of our identity in Him—the sweet spot of the Christian life.

Teaching

In the last meditation, I used the metaphor of the path that leads to Christ and presented the idea that if our identity is found solely in Him, we will keep our eyes fixed on Him and walk the path solely in His direction. We looked at what it meant to veer off the path when we depend on ourselves, grab control of our life, and, in our pride, try to go it alone. Our pride tells us that we can walk through life on our own. Jesus may be our end goal, but we can get there using our own navigation.

As I stated, the enemy wants us anywhere but solidly in the center of the road to which God has called us. He is thoroughly happy if, in our pride, we veer off the path to our left. He is just as happy if, in our despair, we careen off the road to the right. In our leadership pride we believe we can go it alone, and in our discouragement we don't believe we can go it at all. Either way, the enemy is content.

As you read through the nine texts above, I hope you got a feeling for the consistent call in scripture for us not to be discouraged. The common denominator in these texts, and dozens more, is the refrain, "The Lord will be with you." We can only affirm this wonderful truth if our eyes remain fixed on Jesus. As soon as we look away from Him, the challenges and trials of this life can overwhelm us. Even worse, when we look to ourselves to solve our own problems, we too often meet with the kind of failure that can cause us to despair.

In a very insidious way, our discouragement is more of a sign of our lack of trust in God than it is of our pride. The 2 Chronicles 20:15 passage declares, "The battle is not yours, but God's." Do we believe that? Do we believe that the one who leads us down the path of life is the one who has overcome? Do we believe that He has scouted the way, knowing that even the struggles and trials we will face on this path will end in victory because we follow the one who's already won the victory for us? The only way we can know discouragement as leaders is by looking away from the face of the Son of God and letting the cares and concerns of our work rob us of the peace only He can offer.

This is the enemy's agenda—puffing us up in our pride or beating us down in discouragement. Whether we think more of ourselves or less of ourselves than we ought, we become ineffective as leaders in the kingdom of God. There is a sweet spot to the life of a steward leader that far too few of us find. It is that place of stability, balance, and confidence when we are in the center of the path to which God has called us, our eyes fixed fully on Him, and our stride steady and sure in His direction. We find that spot when we deny the enemy the opportunity to lie and deceive us into believing that we can go it alone or to discourage us from going at all.

Where are your feet today? Your eyes? Your heart? Your identity? There is a sweet spot waiting for you.

Action

Think back to the last time you were really discouraged in your leadership role. You may not have to think far. Focus for a moment on the cause of your discouragement. Was it unknown to God? Was it greater than His ability to overcome it? Was it outside of the bounds of His love for you? You know the answer to all of these is a resounding no! So what was the cause of your discouragement?

Try completing this sentence: "I was discouraged because I believed that _____ was too big a problem for God to handle."

Read it to yourself out loud, and if you don't believe it's true, then say so at the top of your voice: "This is a lie, and I'm not going to believe it anymore!" Now take your eyes off the source of your discouragement and focus them fully on Jesus Christ. Open your heart to Him and begin to walk confidently and boldly in His direction. See if soon, and very soon, your heart is changed and your spirit renewed as you reclaim your full identity in Christ and Christ alone.

Prayer

Gracious and patient God, I don't know why I get so discouraged and allow the struggles of this world to become such the focus of my daily life. I know this is not of you. I know you stand and call and wait and hope that I will stop looking at my troubles and start looking again at you. Thank you for your patience. Help me, Lord, through the power of your Holy Spirit, to renounce this spirit of discouragement and to start back on the path that leads to you. These are not small problems, Lord. Some of them seem so big they almost overwhelm me. But I do not believe they're too great for you. I claim the promise that you will lead me through these struggles to a greater victory that I might lead others to the same. I place my trust in you. Please help me put my feet back on the right path. I'm ready to begin leading with boldness and confidence with you as my guide. In your holy and victorious name, I pray. Amen.

Meditation #26

THE APPLAUSE OF NAIL-SCARRED HANDS

Am I now trying to win the approval of human beings, or of God? Or am I trying to please people? If I were still trying to please people, I would not be a servant of Christ (Galatians 1:10).

If the world hates you, keep in mind that it hated me first. If you belonged to the world, it would love you as its own. As it is, you do not belong to the world, but I have chosen you out of the world. That is why the world hates you (John 15:18–19).

KEY THOUGHT

God's love for us and His divine approval is all we need in this world, a world that will hate us as it hated Him.

TEACHING

We all like applause. Be honest—there are few things more exhilarating than a room full of people enthusiastically applauding something you have just done. The sound of applause brings the affirmation that we have accomplished something pleasing, acceptable, commendable, and enjoyable. It signals that we are appreciated by our peers. This kind of commendation can come to us in many forms. Affirming e-mails from friends, a word of appreciation from an employee, a cheer from the crowd at a sporting event, and so forth. Our spirits need affirmation. God created us that way. How, then, do we understand these two rather challenging texts?

Paul sets winning the approval of humans and being a servant of Christ at odds with each other. Jesus takes it further. He claims that if we truly desire to follow Him, then we can expect that we will be hated by this world. So much for applause.

I think both Jesus and Paul were telling us that the greater we love someone, the deeper we will seek after their love and affirmation in return. If we truly love God with all our heart, soul, strength, and mind, will it not follow that His love and affirmation of us will be more important to us than that of all others? This may be the greatest test of where our love truly lies. If our love for God gets lost in our love for other things (acceptance, security, prosperity, happiness, etc.), then we will seek applause from sources other than God alone.

A few years ago, I had a difficult conversation with a pastor regarding his leading of his congregation. In the midst of our discussion, he admitted to me, "Scott, you have to understand that I am a people pleaser." That comment continues to anger me, and I think about how it is played out in compromised theology and lifeless leadership by so many leaders today. When we seek the applause of the people around us more than the affirmation of God, we are through as effective Christian leaders.

We must not read these texts as saying that we should go out of our way to upset people and inspire their hatred. If we focus our lives on serving God alone, and if our spirits are filled to overflowing with the affirmation that we are in His will and doing His work the way He leads us, then we will naturally be put at odds with the values of the world around us. The more we stay true to following Christ, the more likely it is that we will upset and offend those who so eagerly thirst for a broader audience. The "hatred" we will experience will come even in the face of our passionate desire to love our neighbors as we love ourselves. In fact, it just might be the nature of that love that incites the hatred from others.

I have a bookmark that always inspires me. It reads, "It doesn't matter if the world knows or sees or understands, the only applause we're meant to seek is that from nail-scarred hands."

What kind of applause are you seeking today? Whose affirmation means the most to you? Where have you compromised following Christ in order to win the approval of people? And does your work as a leader so passionately align with the values of the kingdom of God that you run the risk of having people hate you because you claim the name of Christ?

Whom are you seeking to please today?

Action

Think back to the last time that living your faith cost you something. Perhaps it was a friendship, a job, an invitation, a grant? If you had to do it over again, would you make a different decision? Likely not. When we are faithful in our walk with Jesus Christ, any related "cost" seems relatively insignificant. Now think back to a time when you compromised your faith in order to either win applause or avoid rejection. If you had to do it over again, would you make a different decision? Likely so. In your journey to freedom as a steward leader, make a commitment today to seek only the applause of nail-scarred hands.

Prayer

Loving and faithful God, I confess to you that there have been times when I chose not to speak your name, acknowledge my love for you, or identify myself as one of your followers. I've compromised in the past in order to please people and gain their applause. Forgive me, Lord, for ever having denied you in even the smallest, most subtle ways. Lord, I need you to strengthen me for this leadership role to which you have called me. I don't like being hated or disapproved by people. Yet I know that the time will come when being a faithful steward leader will cost me in this way. Prepare me for it, Lord. Help me develop a heart that loves you so deeply that your affirmation alone will overflow my spirit to the point where nothing else is needed. Give me a passion for the applause of nail-scarred hands. In your precious name, I pray, amen.

Meditation #27

HUMBLE ON THE STEEPLE

Then the devil took him to the holy city and had him stand on the highest point of the temple. "If you are the Son of God," he said, "throw yourself down. For it is written: 'He will command his angels concerning you, and they will lift you up in their hands, so that you will not strike your foot against a stone.'" Jesus answered him, "It is also written: 'Do not put the Lord your God to the test'" (Matthew 4:5–7).

KEY THOUGHT

The greatest affirmation we will ever receive, the praise that our soul yearns for, will only be ours when we humble ourselves under God's almighty hand.

TEACHING

It is likely that we have heard this story so often that it becomes difficult to figure out just what was at stake in this interaction between Jesus and Satan. When we consider that the enemy only had three shots at knocking Jesus off His messianic journey, we have to take seriously that Jesus really felt this to be a significant temptation. What would've been lost had Jesus taken him up on it? It's not like Satan was asking Jesus to renounce the cross, deny His divinity, or forsake His ministry. So what would've happened if Jesus had jumped off that steeple and His angels had caught Him and floated Him safely to the ground below? Would that have been such a big deal?

Satan was tempting Jesus with an opportunity to be spectacular. Now, Jesus did a lot of things on His own that were pretty spectacular. Walking on water, healing the sick, and raising the dead are certainly no miracles to sneeze at. So if Jesus was going to carry out a ministry that included spectacular miracles, why shrink back from starting off with a swan dive off the temple?

I believe the answer is easy and also incredibly challenging. Throughout the book of John, Jesus tells us that He came to show us the heart of God the Father. He came to speak the truth of who we are as children created in the image of God. He came to show us the Father's intent for us, His love for us, and His desire to redeem us back into a relationship with Him. And He came to be the vehicle through which that redemption would take place.

Everything in Jesus's ministry was meant to point people to the truth that they would know the heart of the God who loved them. Every miracle, every teaching, even every word from the cross had this focus. Jesus was declaring the coming of the kingdom of God. That was His single focus.

A jump from the top of the temple would have denied Jesus's ministry at its very core. It would have taken the focus off the Father and placed it solely on Jesus the Amazing. Jesus's sole identity was the Son of the everlasting Father who came to speak the truth of the Kingdom and the power of the Spirit. A grandstanding event such as Satan was suggesting would have been a denial of that identity. Satan knew that throughout Jesus's ministry, people would want to make Him a king. Many would follow Him because He fed them and cured them, and others expected Him to lead a rebellion against Rome. All of these would be opportunities to deny His true identity and to do the spectacular. At the very launch of His ministry, Satan's temptation brought Jesus to the point of decision.

Satan offered Jesus the chance to be famous, popular, praised, noticed, applauded, honored, esteemed, and recognized. Jesus was tempted to bring notoriety to himself through a dramatic act, seeking the praise of men. In doing so, He would have become an idol, an icon. He would have become the focus of our fascination but not the savior of our souls. Jesus rejected the popularity of the public and refused to fall to the temptation to be lifted up by anyone except God alone.

How about you? Jesus tells us that if we will humble ourselves in the sight of the Lord, He will lift us up. Is that enough for you?

ACTION

What is the enemy offering you today that promises you notoriety, popularity, applause, or fame? In what settings is it important for you to put yourself first, push yourself forward, or make sure that you get the credit you deserve? What activities are you involved in that are more about bolstering your own image than bearing witness to Jesus Christ? These are hard questions for us as leaders, but if we can imagine ourselves sitting in the place of Jesus, confronted by an enemy who quietly and deceptively lures us into such situations, then we can understand the danger we face. Sit down with your leadership team or your closest friend and ask this one simple question: "Where do you see me putting myself forward in a way that puts more focus on me than on Jesus?" If you have the courage to hear the answer, it may be the place to focus on prayer and repentance in the days ahead.

PRAYER

Loving and gracious God, thank you for standing before the enemy in my place and rejecting the temptation to which I so often yield. Thank you for winning a victory over the need to do the amazing in order to bring glory on yourself. Lord, I really struggle in this area. Help me, through the power of your Holy Spirit, to reject all such temptations in my life. Help me lose myself in you, for you promise me I will find my life in that process. Strengthen me for the battle, Lord, that I may be equipped to stand against the enemy's attacks. Empower my life and leadership to be a daily witness to you. Help me affirm with the prophet John that I must decrease and you must increase. Let that be my goal and my joy for my life as a leader from this day forth. In Jesus's name, amen.

Meditation #28

A LEADER OF NO REPUTATION

Let this mind be in you, which was also in Christ Jesus, who, being in the form of God, did not consider it robbery to be equal with God, but made himself of no reputation, taking the form of a bondservant and coming in the likeness of men. And being found in appearance as a man, he humbled himself and became obedient to the point of death, even the death of the cross (NKJV, Philippians 2:5–8).

KEY THOUGHT

God, and God alone, is the caretaker of our reputation.

TEACHING

I love the New King James Version of Philippians 2, especially the phrase, "made himself of no reputation." Now, it doesn't say that Jesus made himself a bad reputation or a questionable reputation, but simply "no reputation." That is, reputation, image, prestige, prominence, power, and other trappings of leadership were not only devalued—they were purposefully dismissed. Reputation—it's cultivation, elevation, and protection—was of no importance to Jesus in His ministry. Jesus became such a man. Not by default or accident but by intention and design. And it was only in this form that He could serve, love, give, teach, and, yes, lead.

This may be a challenge for us, for we have come to believe that the development of a good reputation is part and parcel of living a holy and ethical life. But in that assumption lies an insidious temptation. Reputation and pride are so closely linked that it is difficult for us to consider one without the other. When we are concerned about our reputation, we cannot help but be attentive to what people think of us, be sensitive to criticism, and always be on guard to protect a wrong notion or unfair judgment of our work and character. Here is a rather harsh conclusion I've come to: caring too much about our reputation as leaders is absolute bondage. We can spend the rest of our lives running around propping up our reputations, making sure nobody feels ill toward us and trying to squash any rumor or bad report. And we can do this all the time believing this has nothing to do with our pride. Such is the deception that underlies this idea of reputation.

In reflecting on my life, I have come to believe that following Jesus is an ongoing, disciplined practice of becoming a person of no reputation and, thus, of becoming more like Christ in this unique way. In his reflections on Christian leadership, Henri Nouwen refers to this as resisting the temptation to be relevant. He said in *In the Name of Jesus*, "I am deeply convinced that the Christian leader of the future is called to be completely irrelevant and to stand in this world with nothing to offer but his or her own vulnerable self."[*]

There was a time in my life when I would've rejected this idea outright. Now I believe it is the fundamental position of a disciple of Jesus Christ. Here is the bottom-line takeaway from this meditation: I am not the caretaker of my own reputation. When we can embrace this understanding, heavy chains will fall from our shoulders. We are called to be obedient disciples of Jesus Christ, period. That may bring us a good reputation,

---

[*] Henri Nouwen, *In the Name of Jesus: Reflections on Christian Leadership* (Chestnut Ridge, NY: Crossroads, 1999), 37.

a bad reputation, or no reputation at all. That is up to God. If we obediently follow Him, love our neighbors, speak the truth in love, and proclaim the coming kingdom of God, then our reputation should be of little consequence to us.

Are you leading in a way that ensures the safekeeping of your own reputation? Are you willing to give it up completely in order to follow Jesus regardless of the cost?

Action

Think back to a time when an unjust rumor or a skewed perspective threatened your reputation. How much effort and energy did you employ in trying to "set things straight"? If you were known simply as a person who would go wherever God directs and do whatever God asks, would that be enough for you? If so, then name the first thing you have to do to turn your reputation back over to God. Then place it in His hands with confidence that if you obey Him, He will be the caretaker of your reputation.

Prayer

Gracious Lord, I struggle so much with my reputation. I confess that I want people to think well of me, and it hurts when something damages how others think of me. I don't understand how you could stand to listen to the insults and lies that were hurled at you before you went to the cross and remain silent about them. Sometimes I wonder why you didn't defend yourself, yell out the truth, and hold accountable the people who slandered your name. But I understand that sometimes following you requires us to let people think of us what they may. Lord, I can't do this on my own. I need the power of the Holy Spirit to calm my spirit so that I may rest in you. I give you back my reputation, and today I will walk away from my frantic work of constantly protecting it and propping it up. My only desire is to be a disciple of Jesus Christ, a faithful follower of you, and someone who boldly and confidently speaks the truth in love into this hurting and broken world. Help me focus solely on that and set aside my claim on my reputation. I give it back to you willingly and completely today. In Jesus's name, amen.

Part V

FROM MEANS TO ENDS: THE RELATIONSHIPS OF THE STEWARD LEADER

Jesus called us to love our neighbor as we love our self. The leadership version may be to lead our people as we ourselves are led by God. Here we see the interconnectedness of these seven areas of the life of the steward leader. Owners build second kingdoms to exercise control. They work hard in order to secure the praise of men and tie their identity to their job. As a result, they are leaders in bondage that manage people as a means to the end of their own success. Stewards surrender control and seek to be one-kingdom leaders. They value intimacy with God, from which they derive their identity in Christ. As a result, they are free to manage people as ends in and of themselves.

As leaders we will primarily view our people from one of these two perspectives, means or ends. If we are driven to success by our own bondage, we will look to our people to produce success for our organizations, which will result in our own success. Because our identity is tied to our role as leader, we cannot fail, for failure is not just vocational, it is personal, ontological. So we lead with a sense of controlled franticness as we drive others to achieve our own ends. We don't do this in any nefarious way. But even in our best intentions of leading like Jesus, if we are in bondage as leaders, we will ultimately fall back to our second-kingdom ways and seek our affirmation from the externalities of organizational accomplishments.

Steward leaders are free to be used by God to see our people unfolded into the fullness for which they were created. Such leaders are not threatened by the success of others, nor do they seek to steal their spotlight.

Here is one simple test of which leadership approach most marks your journey. Owner leaders absorb praise and deflect criticism; steward leaders absorb criticism and deflect praise. Which type of leader are you? I pray these next seven meditations will help you on your journey of freedom to engage in relationships that set others free.

Meditation #29

FINDING YOUR FELLOW TRAVELER

Therefore, since we have such a hope, we are very bold. We are not like Moses, who would put a veil over his face to prevent the Israelites from seeing the end of what was passing away. But their minds were made dull, for to this day the same veil remains when the old covenant is read. It has not been removed, because only in Christ is it taken away. Even to this day when Moses is read, a veil covers their hearts. But whenever anyone turns to the Lord, the veil is taken away. Now the Lord is the Spirit, and where the Spirit of the Lord is, there is freedom (2 Corinthians 3:12–17).

KEY THOUGHT

If we pray for it and look for it, God will open doors every day for us to share our freedom with the people around us.

TEACHING

When we lived in Pennsylvania, I had an ongoing battle with crabgrass. One day I found a treatment that eliminated it from my lawn. What is interesting to me is that the rest of the summer I noticed all the crabgrass in other people's lawns. It is like I had a new crabgrass antenna that picked up on everywhere that broad-leafed plague popped up. It seems when we are free of something it becomes easier to see where others are still under siege.

I believe that is true for the children of God who have been set free in relationship with the people we lead and serve. When we are on that journey to freedom, our focus shifts from our agenda, our needs, and our goals. This shift allows us the opportunity to recognize how those around us struggle with that same enslavement. This is not a cause for smugness or pride—quite the opposite. It should engender in us two responses: recommitment to our own journey to freedom and a desire to be used by God to walk with our friends and coworkers toward that same freedom.

When we see our people struggling with old habits, attitudes, and actions, chained by their need to use others to meet their own goals and pursue their own agendas, our response should be one of prayerful preparation. We must surrender ourselves to God and ask that He use us to lead our people on the journey and discover the joy that comes from being set free. Because this is all solely God's work, we can do so with no hint of pride on our part. Remember, you have been set free in order to be used by God to set others free. It is our calling as leaders to be bold and testify with unveiled faces to our journey.

Just how you will go about leading your people toward this freedom will depend on your organizational culture, your leadership style, and how God opens doors and leads you through them. Remember, this is God's work—all He asks of you is to be available and faithful. One way to start is to ask yourself this: "What do I wish someone would have said to me to help me take my first steps to freedom in my relationship with my neighbor?" Answer that for yourself, and you may open the door to the path along which you can take your first steps, watching God set people free through your obedience to His leading.

In an earlier meditation, I stated that perhaps the greatest temptation we face as fallen human beings is the temptation to use others to gain what we want and believe that we need. That insidious desire will damage every relationship in our lives until it is rooted out. I pray you have begun to sense the freedom that is yours in Jesus Christ. When we surrender our life and leadership back to Him, we are able to love our neighbor as Jesus commanded without the need to ask what's in it for us.

Are you experiencing that freedom on your own journey? If so, will you surrender yourself to God that He might work through you as a steward leader to work that same freedom in the life of people you lead and serve?

Action

The image for this series of meditations is that of a fellow traveler. Create an image in your mind as to what that looks like for you. Perhaps it is an image of a backpacker on a mountain trail. Perhaps she is someone riding with you on a train or walking alongside you on a quiet seashore path. Hold this image in your mind as you go through your day and ask God to help you see every person with whom you work as the fellow traveler in that image. Remember, your fellow traveler includes the employee who frustrates you, the board member who challenges you, the competitor who maligns you to your customers, the financial supporter who demands too much of your time, the former employee who hurt you, and so on. These are the fellow travelers in this life journey whom God calls us to love, to serve, and to set free. It will take a heart of total surrender to live so far outside yourself that this miracle can happen. But God is able to work such a miracle in you, if you are willing and open and lead with the heart of a steward leader.

Prayer

Dear Lord, I thank you for the freedom I am beginning to sense in my relationships with the people around me. I have confessed to you that too often I have used people as means to my own ends. My heart aches when I think of some of the relationships I have lost because of my wrong attitude. Now that I am sensing the freedom of truly loving my neighbor because of your love for me, help me to be an instrument of freedom in the lives of those around me. I don't know exactly what that looks like, but I believe that if I remain open to you, you will open the doors and give me the words to say at the right time. Give me courage, Lord, to share with others what you have done in my heart. And every day help me to view every person around me as a fellow traveler, in need of love, affirmation, encouragement, and hope. May each person I lead and serve find that in me, as every day I find that in you. In Jesus Christ, my Lord, amen.

Meditation #30

LEADING THE UNLOVABLE

> *"Teacher, which is the greatest commandment in the Law?" Jesus replied: "'Love the Lord your God with all your heart and with all your soul and with all your mind.' This is the first and greatest commandment. And the second is like it: 'love your neighbor as yourself.' All the law and the prophets hang on these two commandments" (Matthew 22:35–40).*

KEY THOUGHT

We can love our neighbor, and we can understand God's incredible love for us and His desire that we see others as He sees them.

TEACHING

My wife and I have some rental property, and once we had some extremely difficult tenants. Their unfounded accusations and nasty temperaments made for a very uncomfortable and difficult situation. My first reaction was in line with my flesh. Legal action, threats, and poisonous e-mails were the immediate weapons I considered to get my way, protect my rights, and even the score. Looking at the situation through my flawed human eyes, all I could feel was anger and resentment.

Jesus's teaching in Matthew 22 is so common to us we may be tempted to read over it and move on. But we must not miss his rather astonishing conclusion that "all of the law and prophets hang on these two commandments." I interpret that as saying that everything we're taught in scripture about the nature of God and our place in this world can be summed up in these two directives.

The key is the causal link between them. Simply put, if we are passionately in love with God through His son Jesus Christ in the power of the Holy Spirit, we will understand how deeply He loves us. And when we live out of that deep sense of God's love and acceptance, we will give ourselves away in service to those around us. Without the love of God in our hearts, we are thrown back on ourselves to figure life out, which means placing ourselves at the center and looking out for our needs first and foremost. When we do our, neighbor becomes a means to our own ends or an obstacle in our way.

Situations like the one with my tenants bring into sharp relief the worldview by which we live. Through my devotional and prayer times I began to consider two questions; "What is happening in the lives of these people that have made them live this way?" and "This may be the only time our two life journeys intersect, so could I possibly be used by God to help them see in me His incredible love for them?" When I started with God's love for me and understood the freedom I have as a child of God to trust God in all things, my attitude in this situation changed dramatically. I began to pray that somehow God would use me to minister to these people. I began praying for them and hoping that in me they can see the love of Christ and know that that same love is there for them.

It's incredibly hard. My old flesh wants restitution. My new creation wants Christ to be glorified. The latter will win as long as I keep my focus—heart, mind, soul, and strength—on God's love for me and the freedom I have to love myself and to be available for that love to flow to those around me, even those who have done me wrong.

Action

There is likely someone in your organization or life whom you have a very difficult time loving. Okay, let's be frank—even liking or tolerating. As you think about that person, give praise and thanks to God for His amazing love for you. Remember and give thanks for all the sin in your life that He has forgotten, blotted out, and set aside. Remember that He loves you fully and completely as His holy child. Then consider how His unconditional love sets you free to love yourself and accept yourself as His child. In that amazing love and deep sense of satisfaction that you feel in your own position before the God of the universe, think now of this person you have such a hard time liking. See if your heart is not softened toward him or her in a way that allows you to consider how you might relate to them in a new way. Fight that old flesh and let the new creation in you overwhelm your mind and heart, changing your attitude toward everyone around you. As you do, you will model what a steward leader looks like and how that freedom and joy can set others free.

Prayer

Gracious, loving, and forgiving God, when I consider the difficult people in my life it is so easy for me to forget how much you love me, even when I am unlovable. I confess that I have not loved these because I have failed to truly love myself as you love me. Lord, I acknowledge that it is impossible for me to live out this great commandment if I am not daily falling more deeply in love with you through prayer, devotion, worship, and praise. The more I love you, the more your love for me will flow into my heart. Lord, overwhelm my spirit with your Holy Spirit. Fill me with such satisfaction in your love that I can lead as a steward leader and truly love the people whom I encounter, even the ones who drive me nuts. That can only happen by the power of your Spirit, and it is by that Spirit that I give myself back to you in the name of Jesus Christ, my Lord. Amen.

Meditation #31

LOOKING AT THE HEART

Now the Lord said to Samuel, "How long will you mourn for Saul, seeing I have rejected him from reigning over Israel? Fill your horn with oil and go; I am sending you to Jesse the Bethlehemite. For I have provided myself a king among his sons." And Samuel said, "How can I go? If Saul hears it, he will kill me." But the Lord said, "Take a heifer with you and say, 'I have come to sacrifice to the Lord.' Then invite Jesse to the sacrifice, and I will show you what you shall do; you shall anoint for me the one I name to you." So Samuel did what the Lord said and went to Bethlehem. And the elders of the town trembled at his coming and said, "Do you come peaceably?" And he said, "Peaceably; I have come to sacrifice to the Lord. Sanctify yourselves and come with me to the sacrifice." Then he consecrated Jesse and his sons and invited them to the sacrifice. So it was, when they came, that he looked at Eliab and said, "Surely the Lord's anointed is before him!" But the Lord said to Samuel, "Do not look at his appearance or at his physical stature, because I have refused him. For the Lord does not see as man sees; for man looks at the outward appearance, but the Lord looks at the heart."

So Jesse called Abinadab, and made him pass before Samuel. And he said, "Neither has the Lord chosen this one." Then Jesse made Shammah pass by. And he said, "Neither has the Lord chosen this one." Thus Jesse made seven of his sons pass before Samuel. And Samuel said to Jesse, "The Lord has not chosen these." And Samuel said to Jesse, "Are all the young men here?" Then he said, "There remains yet the youngest, and there he is, keeping the sheep." And Samuel said to Jesse, "Send and bring him. For we will not sit down till he comes here." So he sent and brought him in. Now he was ruddy, with bright eyes, and good-looking. And the Lord said, "Arise, anoint him; for this is the one!" Then Samuel took the horn of oil and anointed him in the midst of his brothers; and the Spirit of the Lord came upon David from that day forward. So Samuel arose and went to Ramah (1 Samuel 16:1–13).

Key Thought

If we could see people as God sees them, we would be moved to love them as He loves them.

Teaching

God looks at the heart. I wonder what that must look like? Can you imagine looking at the people in your organization and being able to see deep into their spirits? Imagine seeing more than their outward appearances. What would it be like to be able to see into the heart of the people we work with each day?

We will never have that opportunity, but it is a question and a desire that should guide us in the way we interact with others. The fact is, there is always significantly more going on in a person's spirit than what we will perceive in our encounters with them. The important thing is not that we somehow magically conjure up the ability to look into their soul but that we stay closely connected with the Holy Spirit, who can guide us according to God's knowledge of the heart. That is, it is enough that God looks at the heart so long as He also guides and directs us to respond to others accordingly.

Stephen Covey shares the following story. "I remember a

mini-Paradigm Shift I experienced one Sunday morning on a subway in New York. People were sitting quietly—some reading newspapers, some lost in thought, some resting with their eyes closed. It was a calm, peaceful scene. Then suddenly, a man and his children entered the subway car. The children were so loud and rambunctious that instantly the whole climate changed.

"The man sat down next to me and closed his eyes, apparently oblivious to the situation. The children were yelling back and forth, throwing things, even grabbing people's papers. It was very disturbing. And yet, the man sitting next to me did nothing.

"It was difficult not to feel irritated. I could not believe that he could be so insensitive to let his children run wild like that and do nothing about it, taking no responsibility at all. It was easy to see that everyone else on the subway felt irritated, too. So finally, with what I felt was unusual patience and restraint, I turned to him and said, "Sir, your children are really disturbing a lot of people. I wonder if you couldn't control them a little more?"

"The man lifted his gaze as if to come to a consciousness of the situation for the first time and said softly, 'Oh, you're right. I guess I should do something about it. We just came from the hospital where their mother died about an hour ago. I don't know what to think, and I guess they don't know how to handle it either.'"

What kind of baggage are the people you lead and serve carrying through life today? Are you willing to let the Holy Spirit guide you so that you are ready to minister whenever you are needed, despite the external evidence to the contrary?

ACTION

Today you will encounter a number of people whose hearts are heavy, discouraged, despairing, hopeless, and desperately in

---

* Stephen Covey, *The Seven Habits of Highly Effective People* (NY: Free Press, 1989).

need of a word of grace, encouragement, and hope. Open your heart and ask God to make you sensitive to things you cannot see. Commit yourself today to look, really look, at the people God has gathered around you. For each one say a quick, silent prayer: "Lord is there an opportunity to minister to this person today?" If you seek after the heart of a steward leader, you will be amazed at how many divine opportunities God brings your way. Steward leaders look past the externalities and, with the mind of Christ, look at the heart.

Prayer

Lord of all creation, it is so easy for me to carry out my leadership work treating people only according to what I see. I make judgments too hastily, live with false assumptions, and allow the busyness of my day to rush me past people desperately in need of a word of hope. Lord, create in me an open and sensitive spirit that I may not miss an opportunity today to minister in your name. I know that this prayer will likely bring disruption and inconvenience into my life. Give me the grace and the faith to set aside my agenda that I might embrace your vision for my life. Please, Lord, don't let me miss an opportunity to love my neighbor. Overwhelm my spirit with your Spirit, give me your eyes and your mind that I may be ready to be your hands and feet in this world, even in places I may not expect. I'm here, Lord, use me today. In Jesus's name, amen.

Meditation #32

THE RELATIONSHIPS THAT DEFINE US

Then the King will say to those on his right, "Come, you who are blessed by my Father; take your inheritance—the kingdom prepared for you since the creation of the world. For I was hungry and you gave me something to eat, I was thirsty and you gave me something to drink, I was a stranger and you invited me in, I needed clothes and you clothed me, I was sick and you looked after me, I was in prison and you came to visit me." Then the righteous will answer him, "Lord, when did we see you hungry and feed you, or thirsty and give you something to drink? When did we see you a stranger and invite you in, or needing clothes and clothe you? When did we see you sick or in prison and go to visit you?" The King will reply, "Truly I tell you, whatever you did for one of the least of these brothers and sisters of mine, you did for me" (Matthew 25:34–40).

KEY THOUGHT

What kinds of relationships surround you? You will be remembered by the way you lived in relationship with your neighbor.

TEACHING

Every time I attend a funeral, I end up thinking the same thought sometime during the service: *I wonder what people will be saying about me at my funeral.* It's an unavoidable consideration whenever we are forced to face our mortality. The way we celebrate the end of life tells us a great deal about what we ultimately, truly value in the course of life. I have yet to attend a funeral where family and friends spoke primarily about stock portfolios, strategic plan goals, material possessions, or other so-called life accomplishments. If you listen carefully, the theme at nearly every funeral is the quality of the relationships that were left behind. The setting of a given funeral will tell you a lot about the way the deceased lived. I have been to the funerals of very humble people with little means and no great life accomplishments in large churches with standing room only. And I have attended funerals of some wealthy and powerful people whose mourners could scarcely fill five pews. The reason for both was the value of the relationships they left behind.

Jesus's description of the final judgment from Matthew 25 always unnerves me. He places the greatest value on activities that can too often be afforded the least amount of time and priority. If you ever wondered how seriously Jesus takes relationships, look no further than Matthew 25. It is a stunning reminder that the way we truly love our neighbor, give ourselves to serve those around us in need, and value our relationships as ends and not means all have eternal consequences.

What kinds of relationships surround you? How would your peers describe your relationship with them? How would your employees describe your relationships with them? How would your closest friend describe your relationship?

Action

Write down your answer to this last question: "How would you most want people in your life to describe your relationship with them?" Come up with at least five one-word descriptions of the real substance of the relationships for which you would most like to be remembered. Here are a few of mine: trustworthy, caring, honest, encouraging, and fun. Now here's the tough part, find three of your coworkers or reliable friends and ask them to write down five words that best describe their relationship with you and how they experience you in relationship. Then compare their lists to yours. If you can, discuss the two sets of lists and listen to them as they talk about how they encounter you in relationship and also how they react to your own list. Finally, read the text from Matthew again, look at your own list, and ask for God's guidance in answering the question in this manner: "Lord, help me create the relationships around me that breathe life into these words and result in a life of service to others as you described in Matthew 25."

PRAYER

Dear God, you are Father, Son, and Holy Spirit, and your entire being is defined by intimate relationship. Forgive me for the ways I have used relationships to get what I want instead of seeing in them the true meaning of the abundant life. You created us for relationships with others, and too often I have missed that in my drive to lead, fulfill my own agenda, and secure my own success. In doing so I have left many people hungry, unclothed, and uncared for. Lord, I am not totally happy with how others might see me right now, and if you took me home, I would have left a lot of work undone. Give me a heart to love my people, to serve them in your name, and to care for them for your sake. Help me, Lord, to place the highest possible value of my leadership on the relationships around me, for in doing so I know that I will bear your image in my organization and demonstrate your love wherever I go. In Jesus's name, amen

Meditation #33

RESPONSES THAT SURPRISE

Now Jesus learned that the Pharisees had heard that he was gaining and baptizing more disciples than John—although in fact it was not Jesus who baptized but his disciples. So he left Judea and went back once more to Galilee. Now he had to go through Samaria. So he came to a town in Samaria called Sychar, near the plot of ground Jacob had given to his son Joseph. Jacob's well was there, and Jesus, tired as he was from the journey, sat down by the well. It was about noon. When a Samaritan woman came to draw water, Jesus said to her, "Will you give me a drink?" (His disciples had gone into the town to buy food.) The Samaritan woman said to him, "You are a Jew, and I am a Samaritan woman. How can you ask me for a drink?" (For Jews do not associate with Samaritans.) Jesus answered her, "If you knew the gift of God and who it is that asks you for a drink, you would have asked him, and he would have given you living water." "Sir," the woman said, "you have nothing to draw with, and the well is deep. Where can you get this living water? Are you greater than our father, Jacob, who gave us the well and drank from it himself, as did also his sons and his livestock?" Jesus answered, "Everyone who drinks this water will be thirsty again, but whoever drinks the water I give them will never thirst. Indeed, the water I give them will become in them a spring of water welling up to eternal life" (John 4:1–14).

Key Thought

Are you ready to respond like Jesus to every person you meet, regardless of the situation in which you meet them?

Teaching

I am challenged by this wonderful idea that Jesus saw people in the context of their entire life's journey. It challenges me because so often I see people as people only in the moment of my encountering them and fail to take into consideration the full contour of their lives. I am convinced that God wants us to lead with an openness toward the Holy Spirit working in us that we might be sensitive to the bigger picture that is always going on around us.

The people walking near a well in Samaria would have seen a Jewish rabbi talking to a Samaritan woman of dubious reputation. Jesus could have done what was expected, given a sigh of disdain and showed an unwillingness to encounter someone so much further down the cultural food chain from him. But Jesus saw her need, her pain, and her thirst for water that only He could give. How do we do the same with the people we encounter every day?

I was flying back from a business trip when I encountered a frustrating flight delay that would likely cause me to miss a connection, resulting in an extra night in an airport hotel tacked on to an already long trip. Two gate agents were working furiously to accommodate growing lines of angry passengers who faced a similar fate. After the last person had been served, the two sat behind their computer terminals in a daze.

Fifteen minutes went by and still no plane or update on its status came. My frustration reached a tipping point. I rose to my feet, gripping my boarding pass, and began walking toward one of the gate agents. I would be polite, but my tone would be sharp and my words expressive of just how incompetently I felt the whole situation had been handled. As I moved up in front of the beleaguered woman behind the computer screen, another man stepped forward and spoke before I could.

"Hey, I just want you both to know how much we all appreciate what you're trying to do for us. I know this is a lousy situation, but you have done a great job. I'm going down to Starbucks to pick up some coffee—can I get you anything while I'm there?"

I will never forget the looks of surprise and gratitude on their faces. Nor will I forget the pain in my spirit. I was about to respond in the heat of the static moment, and this man had considered these two women in the context of their larger journey and blessed them. It's a lesson I'll never forget.

You work with people every day who, like the woman at the well and those two agents at the airline counter, desperately need a word of encouragement, of compassion, and of hope. Will you cultivate the heart of a steward leader and be ready to respond like Jesus?

Action

When Jesus encountered the woman at the well, His response was completely unexpected. When that man approached the airline ticket counter, his comments were the last thing anyone expected to hear. Ask God to prepare your heart to do something unexpected today. Look for an opportunity to respond to a situation in the least expected way—which means responding as Jesus would. It will mean setting aside your own agenda, not worrying about getting your own way or justifying your actions, or even accomplishing your goals. It will mean looking at life from the perspective of the other person and responding in a way that meets his needs, not yours. It might be the highlight of your day. Will you pray for it?

PRAYER

Loving and gracious God, help me take my eyes off my own agenda long enough to see the work you would have me do in the lives of those around me. Too often I have gone through life with my eyes focused on my own goals and my heart striving to secure my own success. Lift me out of myself and help me see the ways in which you want me to be a blessing to people around me. Teach me your ways, Lord. They are so different from mine. I will need the power of your Holy Spirit to make me sensitive to those things that I've been blind to in the past. I will need courage to say things I have never said and the faith to set aside so much of myself in loving service to others. This is a huge step for me, Lord. But with you all things are possible. I claim that today in the name of Jesus Christ, my Lord. Amen.

Meditation #34

STAND STILL AND LISTEN

Then it happened, as he was coming near Jericho, that a certain blind man sat by the road begging. And hearing a multitude passing by, he asked what it meant. So they told him that Jesus of Nazareth was passing by. And he cried out, saying, "Jesus, Son of David, have mercy on me!" Then those who went before warned him that he should be quiet; but he cried out all the more, "Son of David, have mercy on me!" So Jesus stood still and commanded him to be brought to him. And when he had come near, he asked him, saying, "What do you want me to do for you?" He said, "Lord, that I may receive my sight." Then Jesus said to him, "Receive your sight; your faith has made you well." And immediately he received his sight and followed him, glorifying God. And all the people, when they saw it, gave praise to God (Luke 18:35–43).

KEY THOUGHT

If we see people as means to an end, we will either use them or view them as an obstacle. If they are ends in themselves, we will love them as our neighbor.

TEACHING

Let's face it—there are people who are just nuisances. They stop us in the hallway when we are late for an important meeting. They call us as we are sitting down to eat. They interrupt us on vacation, ask things of us that seem presumptuous, and generally irritate us. Like the blind man at the side of the road in Jericho, they seem to be a distraction from the more important things in life. When our schedules are full, our goals are challenging, and our time is limited, we go through life with blinders on. And as we do, the last thing we want is someone calling out our name from the side of the road. Especially someone who is needy, who will demand our time, our energy, and a little of ourselves. Can we really afford to stop and serve? Can we allow people to take bites out of our busy schedule like this? Can't we imitate the disciples who told this man to shut up?

To me, the key to this text from Luke 18 is the last sentence: "And all the people, when they saw it, gave praise to God." Think back to your day yesterday. Can you identify something you did that resulted in people giving praise to God? You probably didn't heal any blind people, but that is not the point. The result of Jesus's healing touch was not only the recovery of sight but also a changed life that transformed a blind man into a follower of Jesus. And all who saw it joined him in glorifying God.

We live in a culture that is spiritually blind. There are people in our own organizations who are in desperate need of the healing touch of the savior to open their eyes. He uses us in our role as leaders to be His hands and feet for this work. When we take the time to stop, engage, challenge, love, and invite, we have the opportunity to witness the blind receive their sight. When they do, their new life will inspire those around them to give praise and thanks to God. That's a pretty great way to spend a day.

I believe we could look back over the last week and recognize people who have called out to us from the side of the road. Steward leaders seek to have ears to listen and hearts ready for the Holy Spirit to give them the courage and conviction to stop, love these people, and share with them the words that can open their eyes and set them free.

When Jesus heard the man crying to Him from the side of the road, Luke tells us that he "stood still" to notice the man. What will stop you today? What words will cause you to turn your head, look in a new direction, and engage?

ACTION

I believe we would be amazed and ashamed if we were given a glimpse of the opportunities we have each day to impact the lives of the people around us. So here is the challenge. Pray that today God gives you the courage to share your faith with one person. That's right—ask God to let you hear someone in your life calling from the side of the road out of spiritual blindness. Ask God for an encounter where you can be used by God to open someone's eyes and set that person free. Unless you pray this prayer, you may never hear this cry for help. Do not do this lightly, because if you pray it, He will do it. So trust in the power of the Holy Spirit to give you the words to say at the right moment. Once you do, and when you respond, you will realize the joy that comes when the blind see and everyone around them gives praise to God.

PRAYER

Gracious Lord, I thank you that when I cried out to you in my need and in my pain, you heard me, called me to yourself, and healed me. When you found me, I was that blind man at the side of the road. Thank you for your love and compassion for me. And now you call me to live in this world as you did. Lord, I am intimidated by the thought of sharing my faith with the people in my life. I know so many people who are spiritually blind, but I have never heard them asking to receive their sight.

I know it is because I have never listened. Or perhaps at times I have even asked them to be quiet. Forgive me for that, Lord. I am a follower of Jesus Christ, and so by the power of your Holy Spirit, I ask that you would give me eyes to see and ears to hear the opportunities you bring into my life every day. Help me be a blessing to others and share with them the freedom that I have in you. In the name of Jesus Christ, the one who sets us free, amen.

Meditation #35

YOU FIND OUT WHO YOUR FRIENDS ARE

As soon as the lad had gone, David arose from a place toward the south, fell on his face to the ground, and bowed down three times. And they kissed one another; and they wept together, but David more so. Then Jonathan said to David, "Go in peace, since we have both sworn in the name of the Lord, saying, 'May the Lord be between you and me, and between your descendants and my descendants, forever.'" So he arose and departed, and Jonathan went into the city (1 Samuel 20:41–42).

KEY THOUGHT

What kind of a friend are you? The extent to which you give yourself away in your friendships to others is a reflection of your understanding of the way God gave himself for you.

TEACHING

I love the story of Jonathan and David. Jonathan was the kind of friend any of us would love to have. He risked his life for David, confronted the king, and fled for his life from the hands of his own father, all out of his love for and friendship with David. There are many places in this story from 1 Samuel where Jonathan could've taken an easier road. He could've left David to himself to run and hide from Saul. He could've chosen not to become involved or could've befriended David in a less intrusive way. He could've been a "pot-of-stew friend," as we used to say—that is, someone who is happy to be your friend whenever you have a pot of stew on the stove. But when there's nothing cooking, he's nowhere around.

We have all had pot-of-stew friends. If we are honest with ourselves, we may be just such a friend to some of the people around us. The refrain from Tim McGraw's great country-western song "Find Out Who Your Friends Are" goes like this:

> You find out who your friends are
> Somebody's gonna drop everything
> Run out and crank up their car
> Hit the gas, get there fast
> Never stop to think, "What's in it for me?" or "It's way too far."
> They just show on up with their big old heart
> You find out who your friends are*

Can you think of a friendship you have that is costly for you to maintain? Isn't it the cost of friendship that makes it so rich, so satisfying? We hear a lot of preaching about fellowship, community, discipleship, and relationship. But we don't seem to talk too much about friendship. If we did, I believe we would find that one consistent characteristic of true friendship is the sense of journeying together. When we befriend someone, we commit to walking side by side with that person in our shared journey of life. Even if we are not physically present with one another, we find ways to stay involved, keep connected, and remain engaged in each other's lives. We cry together, laugh together, struggle, disagree, challenge, and comfort each other.

For leaders, these friendships are so important. They provide us with equilibrium and perspective and provide us places

---

* Tracy Lawrence, vocal performance of "Find Out Who Your Friends Are," by Casey Beathard and Ed Hill, recorded in 2006, on *For the Love*, Rocky Comfort Records, compact disc.

of relational safety. In this last meditation on the topic of our relationship with our neighbor, I'm going to leave you with this image of Jonathan and David and pray that you may know such rich and rewarding friendships in your life. They require that you live outside of yourself in service to and love for others. This may be the greatest fulfillment of Jesus's promise that if we will lose our life for Him, we will find our life—the life that is truly life, the life abundant.

Action

Here's your challenge. Get together with three or four people you consider to be good friends. Spend time talking about friendship: how to define it, why it's valuable, how to know it when you see it, etc. Consider the question, "How does genuine friendship reflect the image of God in us?" We have a lot to learn about what it means to have great friends and to be a great friend. See if this little exercise doesn't help you in that journey.

Prayer

Lord God heavenly Father, you have been described as the friend of sinners. In your friendship you not only loved us, came to us, and encountered us where we were but you took our sins on yourself, bore our guilt, endured our suffering and shame, and died our death. You have not only been a friend of sinners, you have been the savior of the world. For that I am so deeply grateful. Let me reflect that love in the friendships around me. Create in me a selfless heart so that I may truly be the kind of friend a friend would like to have. And in this way, let me reflect your image, in which I was created. In the name of my Lord and Savior, and friend, Jesus Christ, amen.

Part VI

From Complacency to Nurture: The Work of the Steward Leader

Steward leaders deal with stuff well. This should make sense to us at this point in our journey. Once we have been set free to lead, we can treat others as ends and invest God's resources in His work as careful caretakers of what God has entrusted to us. Having rejected the temptation to play the owner, we can trust God to be our provider and handle His resources with integrity and grace. This includes our time, our skills, and our finances. It also includes our care for God's creation. All of this flows easily and freely from the heart of a steward leader.

On the other hand, this may be the most obvious place where owner leaders struggle. Again, the problems multiply, from the two-kingdom heart to the misplaced identity to the need to manipulate others and now to the kind of scarcity mentality that plagues owner leaders and all who follow them. For the owner leader, there is never "enough." They complain of insufficient time, talent, people, and resources to be successful. They lead from this scarcity mind-set and treat resources, including creation, as a commodity they can control for their own ends.

One good test is to ask yourself as a leader where your true security lies. We are so tempted as leaders to place our security in human performance and financial strength, and both will fail us. Steward leaders embrace an abundance mentality, believing that God will supply all of their needs according to His glorious riches in Christ Jesus (Philippians 4). They place their security in God's promises of provision and lead their people to embrace that same freedom.

Scarcity or abundance; which leader are you? I pray these next seven meditations will help you discern that answer and guide you in your journey of embracing the freedom of the steward leader who is secure in God as their abundant and all-sufficient provider.

Meditation #36

DIGGING OUT A DEADLY ROOT

Those who want to get rich fall into temptation and a trap and into many foolish and harmful desires that plunge people into ruin and destruction. For the love of money is a root of all kinds of evil. Some people, eager for money, have wandered from the faith and pierced themselves with many griefs (1 Timothy 6:9–11).

Key Thought

Until you dig out the root of the love of money, all other forms of repentance will never fully set you free.

Teaching

In our yard we are plagued with an invasive weed called horsetails. The long, slender tubes look so easy to pluck out. The problem is that they are supported by a deep and intricate root system, and when you go to pull one, it easily snaps off just below the surface. You know that a few days later a new one (or two or three) will rise up to take the first one's place. The only way to get rid of them is with a shovel and a lot of patience. You have to dig deep and completely remove the root structure.

On a recent trip to India, I sat under some powerful teaching on generosity. One speaker drew a diagram of a plant with a deep root system. He circled the roots and referred to the passage above in 1 Timothy. His point was, if in our repentance we continually only deal with the visible part of our sin that grows above the ground, we will never get to the root. Paul identifies that root as the love of money, from which all kinds of evils spring.

Becoming a steward leader requires that we take seriously the entangled root system that exists in our lives and that of our institutions because of our love of money and all it rep- resents. True repentance for a steward leader means doing the hard work of digging deep and pulling out these embedded roots. It does little good to repent of our lack of trust in God to be our provider if we do not also understand that the root of that mistrust is a deep-seated desire to hold on to and trust in financial security instead. We can repent of the sins of envy and jealousy; however, they will never be fully defeated until we dig out the root of the love of possessions and the place they hold in our lives when we compare ourselves to others. We can pray against our pride, but, like these horsetails, it will spring up in ever-increasing ways until we root out our dependence on the things of this world and cut off the desire to tie our image and reputation to what we make, what we're financially worth, and what we own.

Digging out this root system is a never-ending process. However, the more often you dig and the more persistent you are, the fewer the sins and the easier it becomes to keep them at bay. As a steward leader, what are you called to do today to begin the process of digging deeply into the values and culture of your organization to identify the root system that is your love, reliance, and dependence on money? What will it take to remove those roots from your institutional heart and replace them with rich soil in which the Spirit of God can lead you and your people into a new time of trust, dependence, and surrender to God through Jesus Christ?

Action

Try this little exercise to help you identify the roots in your organization. Work with your leadership team and finish this sentence: "We demonstrate our love of money when we..." Write down all the phrases that complete that sentence. Here are a few for starters. "We demonstrate our love of money when we envy what other organizations have, tie our identity to what we own and how much we raise or earn, worry about whether we will have enough money to be sustainable, choose to keep and protect money more than invest and use it in God's work, and invest the majority of our working life talking about it." Will you be honest with yourself and make your own organizational list? That is the first step to digging out the deep roots of the love of money in your culture.

PRAYER

Lord, this is a hard teaching. It is easy for me to deceive myself and believe that we really don't have the love of money in our community spirit. But there is much evidence that we do, that I do. So I confess these roots in my spirit that need to be dug out first. Then there are the roots in our operational life that need the same spadework. We can't do this on our own, because we've spent so much time letting them grow. Through the power of your Holy Spirit, please help me lead faithfully in the hard work of identifying everything in our life that points to our reliance and devotion to anything but you. Help me start with those attitudes that live in my own heart. It's so easy for us, for me to trust in a bank account, an endowment fund, a reserve, or other things that are so temporary. My soul's desire is to trust in you alone. Help me be a steward leader and identify everything that competes with our total surrender to you as our one Lord. And as we identify these roots, as painful as it might be, give us the courage to start digging them out. In the name of Jesus Christ, my Lord, amen.

Meditation #37

WHOM WILL YOU SERVE?

No one can serve two masters. Either you will hate the one and love the other, or you will be devoted to the one and despise the other. You cannot serve both God and money (Matthew 6:24).

Do not love the world or anything in the world. If anyone loves the world, love for the Father is not in them (1 John 2:15).

KEY THOUGHT

Both God and the power of money will demand our loyalty and allegiance. Which one is your true Lord?

TEACHING

Let me open this meditation with a bold statement: if followers of Jesus took these two Bible verses to heart, we would radically change the face of Christianity. Jesus minces no words. We spoke in the last meditation about the need to dig out the deep roots of the love of money, which cause all kinds of evils in our life to spring up. Here, Jesus sets up our love and devotion to money as a rival deity. There is no other place in scripture where Jesus makes this kind of challenge. It is only with our love and devotion to money and material possessions that Jesus deals so harshly. Love and hate, devotion and despising—powerful words.

The apostle John builds on these words and tells us directly that we have a choice between loving the world and loving

God. There is no compromise, no middle position. The love of one makes the love of the other impossible. As steward leaders we stand at this crossroads in almost every decision we make with and for our organization. Whom do we really love? To whom are we truly devoted? By what has our heart been captivated? And how is this evidenced in our daily schedules, our budget priorities, our investment policies, and the disposition of our hearts?

If you wonder what it might mean to love the world, let me share some powerful words from my friend and colleague Jay Link, who writes of the following "caution lights" that should cause us to stop and take notice.

Caution Light #1

We are falling in love with the world…when we are never quite satisfied with what we have [Ecclesiastes 5:10; 6:7].

Caution Light #2

We are falling in love with the world…when the things we own end up owning us [Matthew 6:24; 2 Timothy 4:10; Luke 12:15].

Caution Light #3

We are falling in love with the world…when worry about losing our things is disrupting our inner peace [Philippians 4:11–12; Hebrews 13:5].

Caution Light #4

We are falling in love with the world…when our longing to be there is diminished by our affection for what we have here [2 Corinthians 5:8; Matthew 13:22]. *

---

* Jay Link, *Do You "Love the World?"* (Mooresville, IN: Kardia Planning, n.d.), http://www.ministrywatch.com/pdf/DoYouLovetheWorld.pdf.

So consider this: every decision you make as a leader is a decision about lordship. No matter how big or how small, all leadership decisions are guided by a previous decision we have made about who is truly Lord in our organization—whom we really love and what values will drive us. If you love God, you will hate the power that money seeks to have over you. If you love God, you will reject the temptation to love the things of this world.

What do the decisions you've made as a leader over the last week tell you about who you love and serve?

Action

I challenge you to read the scriptures that Jay used to support these caution lights. Be open to the prompting of the Holy Spirit and see if any of these four lights turn on when you consider the way you lead. Can you construct your own list of signs that you love the things of this world? This is a great exercise for a leadership team or a board. Set aside an hour of a board or staff meeting to talk about this issue. Write down the things that you all agree are indicators of your love for the world. Then make a commitment together to pray against these things, asking God to drive out of your hearts any love or devotion for anything other than Him. It is a supreme act of a steward leader and may just transform your team or board.

Prayer

Gracious Lord, thank you for being so clear even though this topic is such a challenge to me. I don't want to love anything other than you. I don't want our people to love anything other than you. I want to lead them to serve no other master but you alone. I confess my life bears witness to my failure in this area. Help me, Lord, each day to set aside everything that keeps me from you. Drive out of my heart my love and devotion for anything else but you and you alone. I pray you become even more powerfully the one and only Lord in my life. Give me eyes to see where I have failed as a leader and a heart that is willing to step out in faith in a new direction. And help my people to do the same. You alone are my God, my Lord, my Redeemer, and my friend. Help my life to reflect that in all I say and do. In Jesus's name, amen.

Meditation #38

RULING IN HIS IMAGE

Then God said, "Let us make mankind in our image, in our likeness, so that they may rule over the fish in the sea and the birds in the sky, over the livestock and all the wild animals, and over all the creatures that move along the ground." So God created mankind in his own image; in the image of God, he created them; male and female, he created them. God blessed them and said to them, "Be fruitful and increase in number; fill the earth and subdue it. Rule over the fish in the sea and the birds in the sky and over every living creature that moves on the ground" (Genesis 1:26–28).

KEY THOUGHT

We were created in God's image so that we might rule over creation just as He rules over us—with love, nurture, care, and compassion.

TEACHING

As we consider our role as stewards of God's creation, we must wrestle with this text that has been so desperately abused. Genesis 1:26 is written as one sentence for a very important purpose. There is an unbreakable link between God's stated desire to make humankind in His image and His purpose in doing so—that we might rule. Our understanding of what it means to rule over creation is totally defined by the fact that we bear God's image in everything we do. There are some in the evangelical world who treat this text as if there were no link whatsoever between these two parts of the same sentence. This has produced two extreme errors.

The first error is to equate "rule" with "own." We have treated creation as if God said to the first couple, "I no longer own any of this; it's all yours—rule over it and do with it whatever you wish." And so we rule, not as bearers of the image of God, but as despots and tyrants, believing that creation is here simply for us to use for our own desires and good pleasure. Once we believe that we truly own this world, we make it subservient to our own pursuit of happiness. The ecological crisis we face around the globe bears witness to the fruit of this ownership mentality.

The second error is to rule over through neglect. That is, to believe the earth will always be here and nothing we do can change that. So we live a self-centered life and ignore our responsibility to nurture and care for the creation. When we rule over it in a disinterested way, we lose the connection between bearing God's image and His charge to us to rule over creation. The result is similar to that of the first error: a creation that is laid to waste because of our own self-interest and the abdication of our responsibility to be His caretakers.

To avoid both errors, we must always hold together these two parts of this important proclamation from the Creator; we bear God's image as we rule over God's creation. In everything we do as leaders in relationship with His created world, we are to be the hands, the heart, and the presence of the God who lovingly created it and who provides for it every day. It is our humble privilege to be coworkers with God in tending to this incredible planet. When we set aside our desire to own and reject the temptation to neglect, we take upon ourselves the mantle of the faithful steward and steward leader. We lead our organizations in serving as caretakers who rule over creation just like God rules over us: with love, compassion, tenderness, and sacrificial service. That is the only way we can truly bear God's image in our role as rulers of creation.

Action

Imagine that you have created a wonderful little vegetable garden. You have spent countless hours in the hot sun constructing raised beds, installing a watering system, selecting the right soil, and carefully planting row after row of seeds. Your hard work and patience paid off, and the garden is in full bloom. Every day you go out and pick the weeds, make sure the water is working well, and check the fence to make sure no rabbits or other animals can get in to eat your crop. And then you decide to go away for a week. You ask a dear friend to take care of the garden for you while you are gone. To make sure this friend understands exactly what needs to be done, you write a very careful list as a guide. Take a moment and write down for yourself what you think you would include on that list. Be specific: watering twice a day, weeding, checking the fence, looking for bugs, harvesting as needed, etc. Now take a look at that list and ask, as one who has been given the supreme privilege and vocation of representing God in caring for this world, what kind of list has God left you as a steward of creation? How well do you know what is on that list, and how faithful are you in carrying it out as you bear His image in this world?

Prayer

Dear heavenly Father, Creator of the world, thank you for creating me in your image and giving me the vocation of ruling over your world. I confess that I have not often enough considered my responsibility and privilege in doing this work or leading my people in doing the same. Forgive me and us, Lord, when we have viewed your world through the eyes of the owner or with the heart of neglect. Cultivate in me the heart of a faithful steward that I might lead my people as a steward leader. Give me clarity in this vocation, that I may carry out this work in a way that pleases you, serves my people, and bears witness to the world that we are your children. You have left us an incredible gift in this creation—help me help my people rule over it with love, care, service, and wisdom. In these ways, Lord, help us bear your image in this world, because we know that you rule over us in exactly the same way. In Jesus's name, amen.

Meditation #39

THE ESSENTIAL TENSION IN CREATION CARE

And he has committed to us the message of reconciliation. We are, therefore, Christ's ambassadors, as though God were making his appeal through us (2 Corinthians 5:19–20).

Key Thought

We are both one with creation and the King of creation, and we must hold to both if we are to bear God's image in love and truth.

Teaching

In our last meditation, we considered what it meant to bear the image of God as we rule over creation. I want to take that idea a step further. In the creation story, God sets up the tension in which we live as creatures that bear His image within His creation. Here is the tension: we are at the same time very much part of the created world while also being declared the crown of creation. It is extremely important that we understand and maintain this tension, for it is in the midst of it that we serve as stewards in the kingdom of the triune God of grace.

On the one hand, from a molecular, biological standpoint, we are no different from any other part of creation. We are made up of the same atoms and molecules, and we depend on the same air to breathe and food and water to sustain us. Scientists working on the Human Genome Project determined that up to 95 percent of our DNA structure is identical to that of apes and chimpanzees. When we die, our bodies return to the earth like every other creature's does. God chose to create us out of the same dust as He did the beasts of the earth (Genesis 2:19). Most important, this means we rely on the same planet, the same resources to sustain us as do all other creatures on earth. We are united with all creation in depending on this planet and its abundant resources for our very lives and sustenance.

On the other hand, we alone were created in the image of God. While God used the same dirt to form man and beast, is only the human into which He breathed a spiritual life. And it is only through humanity that He chooses to co-labor in this world. Paul reminds us in 2 Corinthians that we are Christ's ambassadors, that God is working His purposes through us. Throughout the history of scripture, God's promises are carried out not by unilateral fiat but through an obedient people. God does not co-labor with the beasts of the field in order to bring about His good purposes and intentions for creation. It is only to us, as the crown of creation, that such a privilege and responsibility falls.

When we lose this tension, we are tempted to worship the creation on the one hand or destroy it on the other. If there is no distinction, we are tempted (as many are) to treat it as sacred. If we overemphasize the distinction and forget our solidarity with the creation, we treat it as a commodity and destroy it in the pursuit of meeting our own desires and seeking our own happiness. Either way, a loss of this tension brings confusion and chaos.

As steward leaders we must hold the two sides of the tension together; we can be stewards of this wonderful creation. We can acknowledge our molecular oneness with all creation and be committed to its care and nurture. As the crown of creation, we can be God's instruments in this world, ruling it and caring for it as His hands and feet. God can truly bring about His good purposes for this world through us if we are willing to be humble and passionate co-laborers with God in the care of creation.

When you think of your relationship with the created world around you, is your viewpoint in balance? Are you leading your organization in ways that honor this tension and engage everyone in a proper view of our role as caretakers of creation?

ACTION

Imagine you are walking on a pristine trail through the forest, and you come across a piece of litter in the middle of the path. Would your response be to say, "Well, if God is so concerned about His creation, He'll send an angel down to pick this up"? Not likely. If God does His work through us, it is important for us to ask about the role He wants us to play as stewards of creation. If caring for creation is our responsibility, we need to have a clear understanding of what that means for us. As steward leaders we can start right where we are. Together with your leadership team (and perhaps your employees, if practical), walk around the perimeter of your property. It doesn't matter if you work out of a downtown office building or a suburban or rural campus, or whether it takes two minutes or two hours to make the walk. Walk around its entire perimeter. As you do, commit the property back to God and claim your responsibility for caring for it. Stop periodically, look at what God has given you to steward for Him, and say, "We are responsible for this." Then make a commitment to do all you can to be faithful caretakers of that property. When our hearts and attitudes are right with the things that are close to home, it is easier for God to work through us to impact our neighborhood, our community, our city, our state, our nation, and our world. Make a commitment today to be faithful in leading your organization in its calling to steward what God has given you. Then see how your people might find other ways that God may want to carry out His work of creation care through you.

Prayer

Lord God, heavenly Father, I give you thanks for this beautiful world you've created. I thank you that I am part of it and ask you not to let me or my team forget the tie that we have with the animals, plants, and all of creation. I also thank you that you created me for the high and holy calling of caring for this creation because I bear your image and work in your name. Help me remember that this is a position of both honor and responsibility. I know you love this creation, and you love me. Help me reflect that love as I lead us in living in this world as your representatives. Give us hearts and spirits that are so malleable in your hands that your will for creation can be carried out through us. And help me lead as an instrument of your peace. Thank you, Lord, for this beautiful creation. In Jesus's name, amen.

Meditation #40

WORK AND WORSHIP

The Lord your God has blessed you in all the work of your hands. He has watched over your journey through this vast wilderness. These forty years the Lord your God has been with you, and you have not lacked anything (Deuteronomy 2:7).

So that the Levites (who have no allotment or inheritance of their own) and the foreigners, the fatherless, and the widows who live in your towns may come and eat and be satisfied, and so that the Lord your God may bless you in all the work of your hands (Deuteronomy 14:29).

For seven days celebrate the festival to the Lord your God at the place the Lord will choose. For the Lord your God will bless you in all your harvest and in all the work of your hands, and your joy will be complete (Deuteronomy 16:15).

When you are harvesting in your field and you overlook a sheaf, do not go back to get it. Leave it for the foreigner, the fatherless, and the widow, so that the Lord your God may bless you in all the work of your hands (Deuteronomy 24:19).

The Lord will open the heavens, the storehouse of his bounty, to send rain on your land in season and to bless all the work of your hands. You will lend to many nations but will borrow from none (Deuteronomy 28:12).

Then the Lord your God will make you most prosperous in all the work of your hands and in the fruit of your womb, the young of your livestock and the crops of your land. The Lord will again delight in you and make you prosperous, just as he delighted in your ancestors (Deuteronomy 30:9).

Key Thought

We were created for work, and when we do it for God's glory, our work is an act of worship.

Teaching

As you look at these texts, you see one common theme: God loves to bless the work of our hands. To better understand this, we need to have a thoroughly biblical definition of "work." Here is a two-part definition: work is a co-laboring with God in the greater work that He is doing, and work is worship.

The understanding of work as co-laboring flows directly out of the creation account in Genesis. When God places the first couple in the garden and commands them to take care of it, He is calling them into a life of labor that is integrally related to God's own work. Paul reminds us that we can plant and water, but only God brings the increase (1 Corinthians 3). As any gardener or farmer knows, growing a crop is a combination of the work we do (tilling, planting, watering, weeding, etc.) and the work God does in providing the rain to fall, the sun to shine, and the crops to grow. In our role as leaders—as well as in every other vocation in our organization regardless of how grand or menial the work may be—we are all co-laborers with God. God is at work in our workplace, and we must see our presence and toil there as a way of cooperating in the greater work that He is doing in our midst. Scripture tells us of God's omnipresence and sovereignty. We must believe that God is active everywhere, even in the hardest of work conditions. God is at work in the hearts and lives of our coworkers, and He calls us and places us in positions of leadership to labor with Him in the greater work of His kingdom.

Our work is also a significant form of worship. If we are to do everything to the glory of God, and if all time belongs to Him, then every minute we spend at work is an opportunity to honor and glorify Him. God created us for work, and when we do it with excellence and joy, our work becomes an offering, an act of worship back to Him.

As you prepare to lead your organization forward, do you see your job as an opportunity to co-labor with God, to enter into the bigger picture of what He is doing in your place of work? And will you carry out your work as a steward leader and in that way transform it into a daylong act of worship? Just as we were called to root out the love of money that we may serve only God and be stewards of His creation, so we are called to be stewards of our work in this twofold way. Are you working nine to five just to make a living, or is your work a reflection of your love for your people and an act of worship to God?

ACTION

Imagine for a moment that you had the opportunity to spend one day in the workshop with Jesus. What would that day be like? It would likely contain a lot of the normal activities of a busy carpenter shop. There would be bent nails, slivers, difficult customers, and crooked lumber. But you can imagine there would also be incredible moments working side by side with the Master, learning from Him, watching Him, and growing in your own skills by being in His presence. I can imagine you would go home believing it was one of the greatest workdays of your life. The truth is that we are invited to work with Jesus every day. How do you see that being lived out in your own work setting? Do you believe that He is present with you and busily at work in the lives of people around you? Do you believe He is guiding your work as a leader, inviting you to co-labor with Him in His bigger work? Pray for God to give you eyes to see the work He is doing, and over the next twenty-four hours, write down every time you see it. See if you're not surprised at how present God is in your work setting and how many opportunities there are to co-labor with Him in that greater story.

Prayer

Lord, forgive me for the times when I have seen my work as a leader as being separate from your presence and actions in my life. I acknowledge that you are very present in my place of work—however, I've just not seen it as clearly as I should. Lord, I want to be a co-laborer with you in my work. You have brought me to this position of leadership, and even in my most frustrating moments, I know that you are with me, present and active in every moment. Lord, help me connect my vision for my work and career with your vision for what you seek to accomplish in and through my place of work. Open my heart that every moment of my life at work may be transformed into an act of worship. And help me lead my people to do the same. I want all of our work to bring you glory. Give us eyes to see and the courage to act that we might accomplish this. Thank you for my job, for my boss, for my coworkers, for my employees, and for the opportunity to serve you in this place. Help me be a faithful steward leader of this opportunity and use me in my work to accomplish your work. In Jesus's name, amen.

Meditation #41

REDEEMING THE TIME

There is a time for everything,
and a season for every activity under the heavens:
A time to be born and a time to die,

A time to plant and a time to uproot,
A time to kill and a time to heal,

A time to tear down and a time to build,
A time to weep and a time to laugh,

A time to mourn and a time to dance,
A time to scatter stones and a time to gather them,

A time to embrace and a time to refrain from embracing,
A time to search and a time to give up,

A time to keep and a time to throw away,
A time to tear and a time to mend,

A time to be silent and a time to speak,
A time to love and a time to hate,

A time for war and a time for peace.
What do workers gain from their toil? I have seen the burden
God has laid on the human race. He has made everything
beautiful in its time (Ecclesiastes 3:1–11).

KEY THOUGHT

God gives us the gift of time that we might redeem it as we invest it in the work of the Kingdom.

Teaching

One of the most challenging topics to study in science, philosophy, and theology is the idea of time. One helpful teaching for me has been the distinction between chronos time and kairos time.

Chronos time refers to the twenty-four hours in a day that is given in equal amounts to every person. We cannot add to it or take away from it. It is dictated by the physical universe. Rich and poor alike have the exact same number of seconds every day, an equal inheritance as human beings on this planet.

Kairos time is redeemed time. When we invest our chronos time in acts of service, love, stewardship, worship, and rest, we transform it into kairos time. When we are driven by the things of this world, the desire to grow rich, the thirst to amass possessions and wealth, the hunger for position, pride, plaudits, power, and praise, we are stuck in a frantic desire to hold on to chronos time. And it constantly slips through our fingers.

Time is one of the greatest gifts God has given us. He put it in place at the beginning of creation, when He created morning and evening. In essence, God created time for us from His very first words: "Let there be light." By creating us in His image, He intended that we fill our chronos days with kairos moments. In fact, it is His will that our entire lives be overwhelmed by kairos time.

The enemy hates kairos time, and he will do everything he can to persuade us as leaders that our demanding role requires us to embrace the frantic, hectic, stressful alternative of a life dominated by the unstoppable passage of chronos time. Which kind of time dominates your life? As you shut out the lights and look back on your day, do you feel like the time just slipped away from you? Do weeks pass with little to point to in terms of memorable moments that will linger in your memory for years to come? How driven are you by chronos time? And how will you create kairos moments?

As steward leaders we glorify in all of God's creation, including time. Therefore, we must fight the temptation to believe we somehow own our time, for the time we own will never be more than chronos time. Instead, we are called to surrender all of our ownership of time and ask God to work in and through us to redeem every moment of it into an offering back to Him. This is a supreme opportunity for us as steward leaders. We must challenge our people to be faithful stewards of time and, seeing their work as worship, lead them in meaningful work that will fill their days with kairos moments. To do so we must model what it looks like to allow kairos moments to take priority over our chronos-driven schedules.

Action

Find a few moments of silence and think back to the week that has just passed. What are the first images that come to mind? A year from now, is there anything that happened in this past week that you will be able to remember clearly, as if it were yesterday? Now think back a year ago and write down two or three memories that come to mind. Why are these so clear in your memory? These two exercises may help you identify what, for you, are kairos moments. Now take out your calendar for tomorrow. What would it mean for you to intentionally seek to create kairos moments in your day? What will you have to set aside, choose not to do, or postpone in order to allow God to fill your day with kairos moments? Is there a friend you need to visit, a call you need to make, a letter you need to write, forgiveness you need to ask for, a talk you need to have with a colleague, a mentoring opportunity you need to follow up on, an act of generosity waiting to be fulfilled? You will have exactly twenty-four hours of chronos time tomorrow—how much of that will you decide to transform into redeemed kairos time?

Prayer

Lord, I confess I have lived my life as if I owned every hour of every day. Time seems to be slipping by so quickly, and sometimes I look back and wonder where the months and years have gone. I realize how much of my life is dominated by attention to the things of this world. As a result, I have had far too few kairos moments in my chronos-driven days. Lord, today I give my time back to you. It was never mine anyway. I pray that you would take this day and help me fill it with rich, meaningful, selfless, and service-filled moments. Please don't let me miss an opportunity to transform a chronos hour into a kairos hour. My time is yours, Lord—show me how you would have me invest every minute of every day in a way that honors you, serves your kingdom, and brings you glory. In Jesus's name, amen.

Meditation #42

THE VOCATION OF THE STEWARD LEADER

For the creation waits in eager expectation for the children of God to be revealed. For the creation was subjected to frustration, not by its own choice, but by the will of the one who subjected it, in hope that the creation itself will be liberated from its bondage to decay and brought into the freedom and glory of the children of God. We know that the whole creation has been groaning as in the pains of childbirth right up to the present time. Not only so, but we ourselves, who have the first fruits of the Spirit, groan inwardly as we wait eagerly for our adoption to sonship, the redemption of our bodies. For in this hope we were saved (Romans 8:19–24). Then I saw "a new heaven and a new earth," for the first heaven and the first earth had passed away, and there was no longer any sea (Revelation 21:1).

KEY THOUGHT

Regardless of how we understand the end of the world, we are called to be caring and compassionate caretakers of God's creation.

TEACHING

Eschatology is the study of end times. Every one of us has our own eschatology of some sort. That is, we all have some idea of how the world might end and what may happen when Christ returns. Unfortunately, these end-time beliefs have provided some of God's people with a ready-made excuse to dismiss any notion of caring for creation. The argument goes like this: If this world is going to be burned up and destroyed anyway, we are wasting our time trying to take care of it. We should be focusing all of our time on more spiritual things. This thinking is both unbiblical and illogical.

In Romans, Paul tells us that the earth itself will be freed from its bondage and fully restored. Far from burning up, it will be "liberated from its bondage to decay and brought into the freedom and glory of the children of God." That view of the new earth is echoed in John's Revelation, when he sees a new heaven and a new earth coming down, showing that creation itself will be transformed through the final victory of Christ at the second coming. From a biblical standpoint, there is no permission or command to desecrate this planet because of some coming destruction.

This argument is also illogical if we were to apply it anywhere else. Would we say of our own bodies that because we will die and our bodies will decay, we should have no concern for them while we're alive? Of course not. In fact, scripture commands us to take care of our bodies because they reflect God's image, just as creation bears God's blessing as He pronounced it "very good."

There is no theology of the end times that gives us the right, the command, or the permission to relinquish our responsibility as caretakers and stewards of God's creation. God will do with this world what He wants. In the meantime we are called to be His hands and feet, bearing His image and working in His name to love what He loves and care for what He pronounced as good.

What does that mean for us as steward leaders? If our

mandate is to live and lead and work as faithful stewards, we have the joyful obligation to look across our organizational life and look for every opportunity to bear witness to this calling. We can apply the faithful steward question across the practices and procedures of our workplace. If we do so with the heart of a steward leader, God will reveal to us the places where we can either stop destructive habits or adopt new habits that live up to this stewarding responsibility and privilege. We do so because we are people of faith and people of hope. When we are stewards of our time, our possessions, and the world itself, we bear witness to our faith in a God who created and sustains all things. The life of the steward is a life of faith. When we live as faithful stewards in all areas of our life, we demonstrate our hope in the coming of the kingdom of God. The life of the steward makes the invisible kingdom of God visible.

This is our high and holy calling. This is the vocation of the steward leader. We are people of faith, people of hope, stewards of all of life, and children in the kingdom of the triune God of grace. To God be the glory.

ACTION

Read Revelation 21–22. Close your eyes and see the whole scene unfold in your mind. The imagery is so rich and powerful. It is replete with rivers and trees, lights, healing, joy, peace, and glory. This is the heart of the God we serve. This is His attitude and His intention for us. It is in His name that we live in this present world, waiting for the fulfillment of all things. Every action you take as a steward leader will either affirm your love for and commitment to this God and His vision or it will deny that faith and side with the one who would destroy the world and all who live in it. As we discussed before, every decision we make in our work as leaders is the decision of lordship.

Make a decision today to be a faithful steward leader who lives a life of faith and hope. Help your people hold this image from Revelation in your organizational mind: it is your heritage, your future. And as you do, pray that God will give you the strength and the courage to be a faithful steward of all of life until you hear these words from the Master's lips: "Well done, good and faithful steward."

Prayer

Heavenly Father, what an amazing future you have prepared for us. Sometimes I forget how deeply you desire for us to be in your presence in your holy city, worshiping you in freedom and joy. I'm so looking forward to that day. Help me, Lord, to live and lead in the meantime in a way that reflects my faith and hope in you. Equip me to encourage and empower our people to live as faithful stewards in every area of our organizational life. I believe your kingdom has already come, and as I allow you to live through me, I pray that the people I lead and serve catch a glimpse of that kingdom. That is how I want to lead, as one through whom the kingdom of God in all its glory can be seen day by day. That's an amazing vision for my life, as a steward leader, Lord. I give myself back to you, surrender myself completely to you, that I may live such a life for your sake and your glory. In Jesus's name, amen.

Part VII

FROM APATHY TO WARRIOR: THE BATTLE OF THE STEWARD LEADER

In each of the previous six areas, we have cited the role the enemy seeks to play in deceiving and ultimately destroying us as leaders. As we come to this final set of meditations, it should not surprise us that we will end by recognizing that the journey of the faithful steward leader is a spiritual battle. In fact, it is the great spiritual battle of our lives. If the enemy can take down leaders, he can bring dishonor to the name of Jesus and damage the witness of God's people. He can frustrate the work of the kingdom and fracture the fiber of relationships in the community of believers. There is so much at stake in the work of the Christian leader, and the enemy knows it.

Therefore, we must end with a series of meditations that help gird us for battle in the full knowledge that the victory is already won in Christ Jesus. There are two brief thoughts for you as you enter this final week.

First, perhaps the enemy's greatest victory has come in his ability to deceive followers of Jesus into denying that there is any real battle at all. If we, as leaders, do not take this battle seriously, we have already lost. We must never get caught in such complacency with regard to a battle that cost Jesus his very life.

Second, even at this last moment we are faced with the choice of being an owner leader or steward leader. In the former, we will attempt to fight this battle with our own strength. And we will fail. We must watch for every instance where we might be striving to engage the enemy on our own terms. As steward leaders we know the battle belongs to the Lord, and in His strength and power we too will see "Satan falling like lightning from the sky." (Luke 10:18)

My prayer for these last seven meditations is that they might strengthen you for this battle and encourage you with the promise that "greater is He that is in you than he that is in the world." (1 John 4:4)

Meditation #43

Prepared and Engaged

The thief comes to steal and destroy, but I have come that they might have life, and have it abundantly (John 10:10).

Key Thought

We must not deny or ignore the fact that if we are followers of Jesus Christ living in this world, we are engaged daily in a great spiritual battle.

Teaching

There are two great forces at work in the universe. One seeks to give us life, freedom, and peace. The other seeks to steal our peace, enslave us, and destroy our life. We live in a world at war whose outcome is already determined. That does not make the battle any less real or the enemy any less powerful or threatening. In fact, the certainty of the outcome serves only to infuriate and motivate the enemy to deceive us all the more. He wants as much collateral damage as possible.

The most heinous form of this deception is the enemy's power to convince us that there is no real battle going on at all. Many leaders are uncomfortable talking about things like warfare, weapons, battlefields, and victory. "Onward, Christian Soldiers" has become a forgotten hymn from a bygone age. Such is the power of this deception. And it will continue to blind us as long as God's people refrain from reading God's word.

You see, the Bible is a book about warfare from beginning to end. There was warfare before creation, warfare in the garden, warfare throughout the Old Testament, warfare surrounding the birth of Jesus, warfare during His entire ministry, warfare in Gethsemane, warfare on the cross, warfare at the founding of the church, warfare throughout Acts, warfare that followed Paul, and warfare right down to the last chapter of Revelation. To deny the spiritual battle we face, we must ignore major tracts of scripture, close our ears to a significant amount of Jesus's teachings, and reject a central theme of human experience that is lived out from Genesis to Revelation.

If warfare and our spiritual battle is such a central theme to God's story of creation, salvation, and final glory, how prepared are you to enter into the battle as a steward leader on behalf of your people?

The aspect of this warfare that concerns us most specifically as leaders is the battle for our freedom. Paul tells us, "It is for freedom that Christ has set us free. Stand firm, then, and do not let yourselves be burdened again by a yoke of slavery" (Galatians 5:1). That is the strategy of the enemy, to re-enslave you in your leadership work even after you have been set free. He does it by lying to us about our relationship with Christ, our true identity, our need to succeed, the importance of our agenda, the value of reputation, and the purpose of our role as a leader. He uses our ignorance and inattentiveness against us. When we lose sight of God's word and become distracted by the challenges of our role, we are easy prey for the lies and lures of the hater of our souls.

God calls us to put on His full armor and wade into this battle. We must fight against the forces that seek to enslave us again. God created us for freedom. Christ set us free. And by the power of the Holy Spirit, we protect and advance that freedom as the army of the kingdom of God. If we shrink back from battle language, we have already lost the war.

It is for freedom that Christ has set you free. That freedom must be fought for every day. That is the calling of the steward leader who has been set free to lead. We must take up our cross and wade into the battle knowing we will be victorious, because greater is He that is in us than he that is in the world (see 1 John 4:4).

Are you engaged in this great cosmic battle? Are you prepared for it?

ACTION

Read through the following passages: 1 Timothy 1:18–19; 2 Timothy 2:1–4; 2 Corinthians 10:3–5; 1 Thessalonians 5:5–8; 2 Corinthians 6:3–7; Ephesians 6:10–20; 1 Chronicles 5:20; Judges 7:20–21; Romans 13:3–5; Hebrews 11:33–34; 1 John 3:8–9; and Romans 13:11–14. What do they tell you about spiritual warfare, our role as leaders, and God's promises? How will that change the way you approach each day?

PRAYER

Gracious and loving heavenly Father, thank you for having won for me the great victory over death and evil. I claim that victory for my life in the name of Jesus Christ. I know that even though the outcome is determined, I am still to be engaged in the battle every day. I confess that I don't feel prepared or equipped to do so. My faith seems so weak that it is hard for me to imagine myself as a warrior. But you have promised that all things are possible through Christ, who gives us strength. I need that strength, Lord, because by myself I will fail in the future as I have in the past. I am sensing the freedom that you want for me. I have felt the chains fall off me throughout this study. I have experienced my anxiety and fear turning to trust and peace. I don't want to lose this, Lord. I don't want to go back and be enslaved again by all of the burdens that I used to carry. So I am willing to fight, to be part of the army of the kingdom of God, to enter into the battle in your name. But I will do so only through your power and with the strength that comes from you. Prepare me, Lord, for this work. Grant me the courage to step out boldly and, with faith, claim the victory of the steward leader in your name. Amen.

Meditation #44

Two-Handed Leadership

To the Jews who had believed him, Jesus said, "If you hold to my teaching, you are really my disciples. Then you will know the truth, and the truth will set you free." They answered him, "We are Abraham's descendants and have never been slaves of anyone. How can you say that we shall be set free?" Jesus replied, "Very truly I tell you, everyone who sins is a slave to sin. Now a slave has no permanent place in the family, but a son belongs to it forever. So if the Son sets you free, you will be free indeed" (John 8:31–36).

Key Thought

The more we seek to live as free, joyous stewards in this world, the greater we will experience the spiritual battle for the kingdom of God.

Teaching

It may seem odd and even out of place to talk about a steward as a warrior. The images we hold of a steward might be that of a servant; an open hand; a smiling, generous spirit. These don't mesh well with images of war: swords and shields, helmets and conflict. But that is exactly the point. There may be no more demanding a journey than the one that beckons us to lead in this world as a free, joyful, surrendered, and selfless steward. That it is exactly the kind of leadership God calls us to. The closer we get to it, the greater will be the enemy's attempts to lure us away.

If we don't take this seriously, we will find ourselves putting on the same heavy chains over and over again. We may have momentary victories that allow us to feel the relief of the freedom of God, but they will not last. The freedom we have in Christ must be maintained by the daily spiritual disciplines that frustrate the enemy and render him impotent. Remember, the greater the impact of our victory as steward leaders, the more determined the enemy will be to steal it from us.

None of this should cause us fear, anxiety, or dread. In fact, we should feel exactly the opposite. When we wage battle against the enemy from the position of this newfound freedom, it is a joyous confrontation. The enemy's weapons against you are deception, fear, greed, pride, and apathy. As a faithful steward leader, you can look at each one and rejoice in your spirit at the victory that God has worked in you. You can look at your feet and see where the chains have fallen. You can stand tall, breathe deep, and feel every moment that exhilarating sense of freedom from the shackles that bind you no more. A heart that has been set free is a heart ready for battle.

The only thing the enemy needs to win back the ground he's lost is for you to deny that you're in any great battle at all. My prayer is that as you enter the final stretch of this journey, you realize that the freedom you are experiencing is a very precious gift. You have done the hard work of identifying your chains, repenting of attitudes and actions that kept you bound, surrendering every area of your life back to Christ, and relying on the power of the Holy Spirit to set you free to lead. After all of this hard work, you should have an even greater determination never to go back again. Apathy can only win when we forget the price that was paid to win our freedom.

From this day forward, I pray that you hold in your mind this image of yourself as a faithful steward leader: one hand always open, sharing generously and freely with joy, while the other hand grasps firmly onto the powerful sword of the Spirit. I am convinced that the kingdom of God desperately needs a new army of steward-leader warriors!

ACTION

As you look back over the journey we have taken, identify one or two specific chains that you found hardest to take off. Where was the struggle greatest, and where was the victory the sweetest? That would be a great place to start as you put on the mantle of the steward-leader warrior. It is likely the place where the enemy will spread his lies in order to take back that ground he has held in your heart for so long. Name it, identify it, write it down if you need to, and make it a part of your daily devotional life to come against the enemy and all his schemes and ways in this particular area of your life. Ask members of your leadership team to hold you accountable and build for yourself some checks and balances to make sure that you move ahead and not backward in this battle. Remember, in the power of the Holy Spirit, the enemy has no chance. The victories you have won on this journey can be yours for the rest of your life. But you must start today to embrace the call of the steward-leader warrior.

PRAYER

Dear Lord, you are the King of kings and Lord of lords. I thank you for the victories that I have realized along this journey. You know when we started how enslaved I was in so many areas of my life. Slowly, lesson by lesson, prayer by prayer, you have worked in my heart to set me free. I know that I have a long way to go. I can still feel the chains in my life where I have not yet surrendered my leadership fully to you. The journey is far from complete, but the road we have already traveled is amazing. As I look ahead, Lord, please do not let me lose any of the ground that I have gained. Give me an image of myself as a warrior in this battle. Help me never to rely on my own strength, skill, or wisdom. It was just such a reliance that got me into this mess in the first place. Instead, let me daily surrender myself so completely to you that, as you promise in scripture, the battle belongs to you. In that I take great comfort and joy. Lead on into the battle, and I will faithfully follow. In the name of Jesus Christ, the victor triumphant, amen.

Meditation #45

NAMING THE ENEMY

Put on the full armor of God, so that you can take your stand against the devil's schemes. For our struggle is not against flesh and blood but against the rulers, against the authorities, against the powers of this dark world, and against the spiritual forces of evil in the heavenly realms. Therefore, put on the full armor of God, so that when the day of evil comes, you may be able to stand your ground, and after you have done everything, to stand (Ephesians 6:11–13).

KEY THOUGHT

The journey of the faithful steward involves a spiritual battle against the forces that would keep us in bondage and render us ineffective as citizens of the kingdom of God.

TEACHING

I was not raised in a church tradition that talked much about spiritual warfare. I'm not sure we knew what to do with Ephesians 6. In developing the theology of the steward leader, however, it has become abundantly clear that living for Christ as a steward leader places us in the very center of a fierce spiritual battle that we dare not ignore. The greatest battle of our lives is played out in the struggle between the owner leader and the steward leader, between submission and control, between bondage and freedom. It is a serious, life-and-death battle because it is ultimately the battle for lordship.

If we recognize the seriousness of this battle, we will take with equal seriousness the call to put on the armor of God. This armor is necessary because when we are dealing with issues of lordship, trust, total submission, and freedom, we are advancing against the enemy's agenda at its very core. These are not little border skirmishes that are merely nuisances or inconveniences in life. These are true spiritual battles, and we fight them every day as leaders in the name of the one who is already victorious.

The freedom God has for you in your journey over the remainder of this fifty-day process will only come through your willingness to engage in this battle. You must take seriously how desperately the enemy wants you to remain in bondage. You must understand that fear, anxiety, and doubt are the fruit of his handiwork in your life. You must acknowledge that each day he whispers in your ear those same words that he spoke in the garden—inviting you to grasp control and play the lord.

The first step toward victory is acknowledging that you are in the battle.

Action

Continue reading Ephesians 6:14–20. Think through what it means for you in your leadership role to put on the armor that is listed there: the belt of truth, the breastplate of righteousness, the boots that are the gospel of peace, the shield of faith, and the helmet of salvation. As you think about the armor that you bear today, where are you most vulnerable? Choose one item of your spiritual armor and pray today that God will strengthen you in that area "so that when the day of evil comes, you may be able to stand your ground, and after you have done everything, to stand."

Prayer

Almighty God and heavenly Father, I don't always see myself as a warrior engaged in a great battle. I have to confess I'm not really comfortable with this language or image. I'd like to think that this battle doesn't exist. Thank you for reminding me just how important it is to acknowledge the spiritual warfare that is everywhere in our world. As a leader I want to be ready, prepared, and equipped for the battles into which you call me. Right now I know there are areas in my life where I am vulnerable. I confess those to you and ask today that you strengthen me in precisely these areas. This is your battle, Lord, fought in your name with the weapons that you grant us. And I know that, because of the cross, the outcome is already assured. Fit me for the battle, Lord. In Jesus's victorious name, amen.

Meditation #46

Proclaiming Freedom

A word fitly spoken is like apples of gold in settings of silver (Proverbs 25:11).

Key Thought

We may never know the incredible things that God will do through us in the lives of the people we meet unless we are willing to be used by Him to set other people free.

Teaching

You may not know the name Monseigneur Bienvenu, the Bishop of Digne, but you very likely know his story. In Victor Hugo's *Les Misérables*, he is the humble bishop who changes the course of history through one act of amazing grace. Jean Valjean comes to him as a broken man, carrying the heavy chains of his criminal past. To make matters worse, he steals from the bishopric, only to be caught and brought back before the man of God with enough evidence to put him away for life. The humble Bishop of Digne not only dismisses the charges but also gives to Valjean the rest of the silver "he forgot." What follows is a beautiful example of the power of grace and forgiveness in the life of a person enslaved by guilt and sin. The closing words of the song that the bishop sings to Valjean in the musical-theater version of the story are these: "You must use this precious silver to become an honest man…for I have bought your soul for God." You likely know the rest of the story.

We have talked a lot on this fifty-day journey about experiencing the true freedom that God wishes for all of His children. That experience is so powerfully demonstrated in the life of Jean Valjean. What we must not miss in this story, however, is the joy and the freedom with which the bishop set him free. Had the enemy been able to enslave the Monseigneur with regard to possessions, fear, resentment, pride, or self-righteousness, the outcome would have been dramatically different. But exactly when Valjean needed to be released from all that oppressed him, God found a man who was engaged in the battle and prepared for the job.

In our prior meditations we prayed for God to set us free in relationship to our image, our self-identity. We sought the freedom that comes from finding our only true identity in Jesus Christ. We set aside the need to prop up our own reputation, and we refused the allure of praise and plaudits. In doing so, I pray you sensed the freedom of the follower of Christ who seeks only the applause of nail-scarred hands.

If you did, now is your time to give it away. Today your life will intersect with people in your workplace and beyond who carry on their spirits the weight of past sins and the burden of self-incrimination and doubt. Will you be the "bishop" to those people—used by God to pronounce a word of mercy, an act of grace, a pronouncement of freedom? You will need to look for it, seek after it, and pray for it. You will need eyes of compassion and the mind of Christ, or these opportunities will pass you by without you even knowing it. But if you let God open your eyes and allow the Holy Spirit to quicken your spirit, you can be used by God in your leadership role as a powerful instrument of freedom and hope. That is the purpose of this entire fifty-day journey to freedom. Not just that we might be set free but that we might be part of the army of God to proclaim freedom to the captives wherever we go. May God equip you for such a high and holy calling.

ACTION

I want to send you back to *Les Misérables* in this action step. If you have the movie or the score, watch or listen to that part I described above again. Be especially mindful of the words and the expression on the faces. Even better, pick up a copy of Hugo's book and read the entire section that tells this story. Then picture yourself as that humble bishop. Remember, he did nothing more than let the love and mercy of Christ flow through him. That is all God asks of us. How powerfully would such a word of grace impact the life of someone you know, someone with whom you work, perhaps someone in your own home? Will you pray for God to use you in such a powerful way through such a simple, humble act?

PRAYER

Gracious and merciful God, I am overwhelmed by the thought that you could use me as a leader to bring healing and hope into the lives of others. I still feel so broken myself. But I trust you, and I am willing to be your person in the lives of the people around me. So I submit myself to you. I don't always have the words or the courage for this. Yet I believe that you can work through me, and so in faith I ask you to prepare me for this work. Then, Lord, open my eyes that I may see the need that is around me. Slow the pace of my life so that I may hear the cries for help that I so often miss. And when I have the opportunity, give me the words to say, the compassion to act, and the heart to believe. Use me, Lord, as you see fit. In Jesus's precious name, amen.

Meditation #47

STRUGGLE AND VICTORY

I want to know Christ—yes, to know the power of his resurrection and participation in his sufferings, becoming like him in his death, and so, somehow, attaining to the resurrection from the dead. Not that I have already obtained all this, or have already arrived at my goal, but I press on to take hold of that for which Christ Jesus took hold of me. Brothers and sisters, I do not consider myself yet to have taken hold of it. But one thing I do: forgetting what is behind and straining toward what is ahead, I press on toward the goal to win the prize for which God has called me heavenward in Christ Jesus (Philippians 3:10–14).

KEY THOUGHT

Our life with Christ is a journey in which we are continually called to walk by faith, grow by trust, and be strengthened through struggle and victory.

TEACHING

Paul reminds us that the Christian life is not a destination but a journey. Following Jesus means, well, following. A few years ago I hiked into the Enchantments wilderness area with my son and three of his friends. The hike is notoriously long and challenging: nearly ten miles with a massive elevation gain. Although I trained rigorously for the trip, it proved a significant challenge for my aging knees and back. We had never hiked it before, so we did not know what to expect around each turn. At one point while crossing a steep area of granite rock and boulders, my hiking pole gave way and I fell, rolling twice through the boulder field. I came to rest on my back, with my backpack shielding me from the jagged rocks underneath. To everyone's amazement, I only suffered a few cuts and bruises. After climbing back up to the trail and looking down to where I'd fallen, I realized what a miracle it was that I had not been seriously injured or killed. My son asked me, "So, Dad, what do you want to do?" I smiled and said, "Press on."

We are focusing on the battle we wage every day as God's leaders. The outcome of that battle will depend on how we respond to the continual invitation to press on. And the deeper we go in relationship with Christ, the more challenging and rigorous the path will become. We were not created to sit on a bench at the side of the road.

The life of a steward leader has both a "pressing on" and a "reflecting back" component. When we descended from our hike, I stopped at the place that I had fallen on my way up and reflected again on the miracle of God's grace. In the same way, our life as leaders has times of striving and struggling, and also times of quiet reflection, considering all that God has done to get us to the place where we now stand. Both of these require continued intimacy with God in the midst of the battle. We strive ahead because we hear His voice clearly and understand His heart in calling us on to steeper terrain. And we will reflect back to the quiet time we create in our schedules to sit at the feet of Jesus and listen. Both our striving and our reflecting bear witness to the level of intimacy that we have with God in Jesus Christ.

Is your life as a leader this combination of striving ahead and reflecting back, or are you sitting on a bench at the side of the road? It all depends on the depth of your relationship with

Christ, the intimacy of the time you spend with Him, and how well you know His voice.

Action

There is a proverb that says, "The journey of a thousand miles begins with one step." So it is with the life of a steward leader. The journey we walk in obedience to Jesus Christ is a day-by-day, moment-by-moment, step-by-step experience. The question we continually ask ourselves is this: "What is the next step of faith God is asking me to take?" Can you identify that for yourself today? If not, you should feel sent back to your quiet time of intimacy with God where you can read His word, listen for His voice, and know and understand the direction from which He is calling you. Ask for the courage and determination to take the step toward God, to step out in obedience and faith regardless of where it might lead you and what it might cost. Know that step for yourself, write it down now, and pray for God to equip you with the strength to take it.

Prayer

Gracious Lord, I confess that at times my walk with you feels as though I am sitting on a bench on the side of the road. When I lose my sense of intimacy with you, I don't hear your voice, I don't understand where you want me to go, and I end up trying to do everything on my own. I come back now into your presence and sit at your feet and wait for you to direct me. I know you will call me onto a path that is challenging, so give me the courage and strength to obey. I also trust that you have things to show me that I will never see if I keep sitting here on this bench. There is a great, exciting, and dramatic life you have for me, one that I will never know unless I'm willing to follow you without hesitation onto whatever path you lead me. Give me that strength, that courage, and that love for you. In Jesus's name, amen.

Meditation #48

SET FREE TO LEAD

Praise the Lord.
Praise the Lord from the heavens;
praise him in the heights above.
Praise him, all his angels;
praise him, all his heavenly hosts.
Praise him, sun and moon;
praise him, all you shining stars.
Praise him, you highest heavens
and you waters above the skies.
Let them praise the name of the Lord,
for at his command they were created,
and he established them for ever and ever—
he issued a decree that will never pass away.
Praise the Lord from the earth,
you great sea creatures and all ocean depths,
lightning and hail, snow and clouds,
stormy winds that do his bidding,
you mountains and all hills,
fruit trees and all cedars,
wild animals and all cattle,
small creatures and flying birds,
kings of the earth and all nations,
you princes and all rulers on earth,
young men and women,
old men and children.

Let them praise the name of the Lord,
for his name alone is exalted;
his splendor is above the earth and the heavens.
And he has raised up for his people a horn,
the praise of all his faithful servants,
of Israel, the people close to his heart.
Praise the Lord (Psalm 148).

Key Thought

The most powerful expression of the freedom we have experienced will be the way we live each day as free and joyous children of God in a world of darkness and bondage.

Teaching

The battle we fight on behalf of creation as steward warriors is being waged right in front of us every day. We don't have to go looking for this conflict—it is brought to our door and thrown in our face almost constantly. From our financial reports to our board agendas to the collective angst of our community, we are bombarded with a sense of anxiety and urgency of getting, and holding on to, money. Maintaining your freedom as a steward leader in this fourth sphere will require daily vigilance. Let down your guard for a moment, and the old nature within you will rise up and entice you to play the owner once again. Remember the words of Paul: "Stand firm, then, and do not let yourselves be burdened again by a yoke of slavery" (Galatians 5:1).

It is not enough just to maintain our own freedom. As challenging as that will be, we were set free to lead our people to that same freedom. The most powerful expression of that freedom will come from how we lead in this area of finances. The great preacher and theologian Charles Haddon Spurgeon said, as recounted by David Jeremiah in *Turning Points: Finding Moments of Refuge in the Presence of God*, "A man's life is always more forcible than his speech. When men take stock of him they reckon his deeds as dollars and his words as pennies. If his life and doctrine disagree, the mass of onlookers accept his practice and reject his preaching."[*]

If you lead in freedom from both the bondage of ownership and a controlling attitude toward possessions and money, your life leadership will get attention. You will lead your organization to make financial decisions that will confuse and bemuse people. You will leave things alone that are addictions to most organizations like yours. You will be more at ease and open regarding your organizational finances than your people think you should, and you will do so with a joy that few will understand. You will create kairos moments in a world obsessed with holding on to chronos time. And caring by the way you lead and the decisions you make will be as natural as loving and worshiping the Creator.

The work of a steward leader is radically different when you operate from a position of freedom in a world in bondage. I pray that you are leading in this revolutionary freedom every day. It is yours as a child of God and heir to the promise of salvation. It is yours as an image bearer of our Creator God and a caretaker of His good creation. It is yours to bear witness to the truth of God's sovereignty over and love for all creation. It is yours as a faithful steward set free to lead.

Claim that freedom for yourself in the victorious name of Jesus. And lead in the power of the Holy Spirit to the glory of the Father.

---

[*] David Jeremiah, *Turning Points: Finding Moments of Refuge in the Presence of God* (Nashville, TN: Thomas Nelson, 2006), p. 18.

Action

If Christ is setting you free in relationship to the things of this world, you should be able to look back at your attitudes and habits before this emancipation and look ahead at a very different landscape for your life as a leader. Is there a stark difference between the two? If not, pray each day for that freedom to overwhelm your spirit and set you free. If there is a demonstrable difference, write down three areas where your newfound freedom is being lived out in your leadership. Then ask yourself if others might see this difference. If so, how can you be ready to give an account for the change that has taken place within you, which has produced this fruit? Seek the Spirit's guidance and be prepared. For if the evidence is clear to see, people will ask. Will you be ready to answer?

Prayer

Gracious God, Creator and Lord, this has been a real battle in my life. I do sense the freedom that comes from surrendering everything back to you and exclaiming with my whole heart, "It's all God's!" It seems like every day my old nature wants to pull me back into my ownership ways. Lord, I pray for a continual transformation of my spirit into a faithful, one-kingdom steward leader. And I pray that as that transformation works itself out, it is evidenced in every area of my life. In some ways that means only small and subtle changes, and other ways the changes are so big they scare me. But you are my strength and my salvation, and in you I will trust. I pray that when the people in our organization look at me, my deeds are dollars and my words are pennies. Let my life bear witness to my true Lord and give me a word to say for all those who ask me to give an account for the hope that is within me. In your precious name, I pray. Amen.

Meditation #49

VICTORY BEGINS WITH SURRENDER

Whoever finds their life will lose it, and whoever loses their life for my sake will find it (Matthew 10:39).

KEY THOUGHT

In the great spiritual battle in which we are engaged, the road to victory begins with absolute surrender.

TEACHING

The journey of the faithful, obedient steward leader is fraught with the same paradoxes as is our journey as a disciple of Jesus. They are, in fact, the exact same journey. In both we find life by losing it, receive by giving, lead by serving, become first by being last, and are exalted by being humble.

In this, our last meditation of our fifty-day journey, I want to leave you with one final paradox: we are victorious by surrendering. How absurd that sounds, but it is the heart of everything we have said over the past forty-eight days. We must understand this simple truth about the battle in which we are engaged if we are to have the hope for victory.

This one truth can be read back into everything we have said:

- It's all God's, and we are called to surrender our desire to play the owner and embrace our role as the faithful steward set free to lead.

- We are one-kingdom people, and we must surrender the role of lord over our own, second kingdom and place everything under the one lordship of Jesus Christ.
- We are given the gift of intimacy with God in Christ, and we must surrender the insatiable drive we have to be doers and allow God to work in us the freedom of the steward leader.
- We are given the gift of confidence, and we must surrender our pride that would have us find our identity and freedom in anything but in Christ alone.
- We are given the gift of presence with our neighbor, and we must surrender the desire to use our people as means to our own ends and be set free to see them as Christ sees them.
- We are given the gift of nurture of creation, and we must surrender the deceptive ideas that we rule creation for our own gain and instead be the caretakers that God created us to be.
- We are called into the great battle for freedom, and we will only be victorious if we fully surrender our will and ways to God, allowing Him to work through us to set others free.

My sincerest prayer is that in some small way over the course of this journey you have come to know the freedom of surrender for yourself. I pray that chains have fallen, lies of the enemy have been discovered, and the truth and beauty of the love of God have been experienced at a deeper level.

May the Lord of freedom be your Lord and deliverer, your strength and your comfort for the battle that lies ahead. And every day may you know the peace that comes from the unchained life and the joy that flows from the heart that is genuinely free.

Action

This final action takes us back to the beginning. Go look again at that jar of dirt you filled about fifty days ago. Remember its message: "It's all God's!" These words started our journey. Now, at its end, I hope they have a deeper and richer meaning for you. They are words of ultimate and absolute freedom. They are words that engage us in the battle for the truth of the kingdom of God. They are words that keep at bay the desire to take the jar back and say, "Mine." They are words that bring life and purpose and hope. Keep your jar close at hand, and whenever the enemy whispers his lies to you about what is yours, who you are, and how you should live with your neighbor and creation, lift the jar high and proclaim those victorious words: "It's all God's!"

Prayer

Gracious Lord, I am coming to the end of this fifty-day journey to freedom. Thank you for walking with me through these meditations. Thank you for all of the moments I felt the chains fall from my shoulders and a true sense of freedom overwhelmed my spirit. Lord, I don't want to go back. I don't want to take up those old chains and carry them around anymore. I know the secret to continued freedom is continued surrender. And so I give myself back to you today: everything I am, everything I say, everything I think, and everything I do. Nothing on this earth is mine, yet you give me everything I need. What an amazing love! I pray, Lord, that you fill me with the power of your Holy Spirit so that I might love and lead others, myself, and this beautiful creation in that same amazing way. I love you, Lord, and I claim this day as my independence day in the name of your Son and my Lord and Savior, Jesus Christ, who came that I may know this freedom, embrace this truth, and let it set me free. I claim the promise that when the Son sets me free, I will be free indeed. In His precious name, I pray. Amen.

Meditation #50

THE CHARGE OF THE STEWARD LEADER

I would like to share with you two closing thoughts. The end of these fifty meditations brings you to a new vantage point from which you can look back over the trail you have traversed and ahead to the path that lies in front of you. Both looking back and looking ahead are important at this specific point in time in your life.

Start by looking back.

As you stand on a rock outcropping, you have a chance to look down over the long, winding path that tells the story of your life. You can see the places where the path was wide, the grade was easy, and the views were pleasant. You can see the places where the path grew steep and narrow, where the view ahead provided little inspiration, and there seemed to be danger on every side. You can see the places where you wandered off the path, got lost in the woods for a while, and finally found your way back. You can remember the places where you slipped and fell, possibly even rolling down the mountain a ways. The cuts and bruises, the scars and pain are still strong in your memory. Looking down on the path you've traveled will also bring to mind the places where you needed help. You can see the spots where others came to help you along. Perhaps balancing you as you crossed a log spanning swift water. Perhaps picking you up when you fell, or perhaps, at the key moment, pointing you in the right direction after you had gotten lost. All of these experiences mark the trail that is your life. Hopefully, part of this view includes a look back to where you were at the beginning of these meditations. As you do I hope you will see that some of the fear, worry, stress, and anxiety that weighed you down like heavy chains has fallen off and now lies discarded at the side of the road. Now that you have reached this viewpoint, I pray that you're able to see and understand a little better all the ways in which those chains have made this path more difficult.

Our attitude toward the path behind us is critical. I would encourage you to consider that God asks three things of us at these times of looking back. *First*, He asks us to learn. As you consider this trail behind you, pray that God will grant you the wisdom to learn the lessons He planned for you along the way. Not one moment of our past life is wasted. God uses all of our experiences to help us become the people He created us to be. There are lessons on every leg, perspectives in the pain, and wisdom to be gained even from the most seemingly senseless times of our journey. Don't let one step of your past life be lost. Seek God's guidance for what He would teach you, remembering that He was walking beside you every step of the way.

Second, God asks us to look back on our lives with a deep sense of gratitude. Do you see God's amazing hand of love, grace, provision, and favor in your life? Even in the hard, lost, and loneliest times, do you see how He always brought you back to a place of safety and hope? When we consider God's amazing presence and provision for us along our life's journey, it should cultivate in us a deep sense of gratitude and thanksgiving that should carry us well on the journey ahead.

Finally, in this looking back, God asks us to leave behind what should be left behind. I pray that through these meditations you have experienced the amazing freedom that God has for His people. You've felt chains fall, you've set aside old attitudes and perspectives that weighed you down, and you've quit listening to the enemy and the lies that used to bind you. Now is the time to take that newfound freedom and move ahead with a clear conscience. This will require rejecting any feelings of regret. It means quieting the voices that want to pull you back into your past where all those chains lie waiting to be picked up and worn again. That is not the life God has for you. As you prepare to look ahead, you must let the past be the past, only taking with you the lessons that will help you in the future and a deep sense of gratitude for the God who never left your side.

Now turn from this viewpoint and gaze at the path that lies ahead. It may seem just as steep and narrow as the one that you just left. You know it will take you through deep forests where sometimes the trail will be hard to follow. You know there will be times when you will need people beside you to pick you up when you fall, to steady you as you wade through fast-moving water, and to encourage you when the path seems too steep. You also know there will be days of trekking through open meadows strewn with wildflowers with the warm sun shining down. There will be places of breathtaking beauty, and sections where you will see the path as far as the horizon with clarity and hope. I believe that, just as in our looking back, there are three things that God wants of us as we consider the path that lies ahead.

First, just as He desires for us to have a heart of gratitude in looking back, so He expects us to start the journey ahead with that same heart. This time it is a heart that anticipates the good things that God is already doing. Do you believe that God has prepared this path ahead of you? Do you trust that He is leading you into experiences meant for your good? Do you trust your God, and if so, can you already today praise and thank

Him for all the steps that will mark your journey from this day forward? Starting this new journey with a heart of gratitude is a way of acknowledging God's absolute sovereignty over every moment of your life. It is your declaration of independence from worry and stress and fear that come from believing that somehow in the future God will be less present, less gracious, less trustworthy than He was in the past. Start your new journey with a heart of thankfulness in anticipation of the amazing things that God is about to do in your life.

Second, surround yourself with great walking companions. Give them permission to speak with authority into your life every time they see you stooping down to pick up a chain. Ask them to remind you of how heavy the weight was when you carried it all those years. Find fellow travelers who can provide you with encouragement, challenge you in love, and help you laugh a lot along the way.

Finally, walk the rest of this journey with a very light pack. Live your life nimbly with an agility that allows you the freedom to find others who are struggling along the way and come to their side. Every day you will walk with people who bear the chains that you have shed. Now you can help the people around you with prayer and encouragement that they would know the freedom of the faithful steward. Ask God for eyes to see them, for a heart to love them, for opportunities to encounter them, for courage to speak to them, for wisdom to guide them, and for the power of the Holy Spirit to work through you as His agent of freedom.

Your new journey begins now. My prayer is that when you reach the next great outcropping from where you can look back over the trail behind, you will see a different, more joyful and fulfilling journey than at any other point in your life. Embrace the journey, claim the freedom, and be ready for the awesome life that God is about to unfold in front of you. Welcome to the journey of the faithful steward set free to live and lead for Christ. God bless you.

Prayer of the Steward Set Free to Live

Lord, forgive my rush to perform that has distanced me from true intimacy with you;

Lord, forgive the imbalance that I have allowed to take hold in my understanding of

who I am in you;

Lord, forgive my use of relationships for my own means;

Lord, forgive my poor use of time and my lack of care for your wonderful creation;

Grant me a heart that daily hungers and thirsts for authentic intimacy with you;

Help me see myself as you see me and give me deep contentment with that view;

Grant me a passion to love my neighbor and a willing heart to be present with them;

Grant me the wisdom to use my time, talents, and resources to build your kingdom,

and the heart of a true steward of your beautiful creation.

In the name of the one who sets us free, Jesus Christ our Lord, amen.